SOUTH AFRICAN BIBLIOGRAPHY

SOUTH AFRICAN BIBLIOGRAPHY

A Survey of Bibliographies and
Bibliographical Work

REUBEN MUSIKER
M.A., B.Sc., Lib.Dip., F.S.A.L.A.
Deputy Librarian, Rhodes University,
Grahamstown, South Africa

ARCHON BOOKS
HAMDEN CONNECTICUT

Published in the United States of America by
Archon Books, The Shoe String Press, Inc.
995 Sherman Avenue, Hamden, Connecticut 06514.

First published 1970

ISBN 0 208 00391 6

Made and printed in Great Britain by
Bristol Typesetting Company Ltd. Bristol

Foreword

In his Introduction to Sidney Mendelssohn's *South African Bibliography* Ian Colvin remarked that although the first voyage round the Cape took place about the time that printing was invented, the literature relating to Southern Africa during the subsequent four centuries had only been half explored. True, the *Klare Besgryving van Cabo de Bona Esperança*, published in Amsterdam in 1652, the year of Jan van Riebeeck's pioneering settlement at the Cape, contained in its margins many references to voyages and travels of the preceding century – possibly the first South African bibliography to appear in print. Likewise, the traveller John Barrow, in an article in the *Quarterly Review*, December 1812, mentions that 'a barren nook of the Southern extremity of this huge continent has furnished even our humble collection with near forty volumes, twelve of which are goodly quartos; and we verily believe that we could enumerate as many more'. But especially in more recent times the volume of material relating to South Africa has swelled to gargantuan proportions. In the first attempt to compile a full *catalogue raisonné* Sidney Mendelssohn amassed more than 7,000 entries, but even so there were many omissions, notably the incomparable collection of early Cape pamphlets forming part of the South African Library in Cape Town itself.

In recent years the Mendelssohn Revision Project, of which I had the privilege of being a founder and first Editor-in-Chief, has discovered more than 34,000 main entries held by South African libraries alone, and a similar number of references from variant headings, all within the period ending in 1925. The need for identification and control of this large and variegated literature is self-evident, and it is encouraging to note the enthusiasm with which this task has been tackled by

Reuben Musiker and many of his colleagues in the biblio-graphical field. It is also appropriate to commend the South African Government for essential financial support, through its Research Councils, in this important work.

Much remains to be done, as Mr. Musiker's survey makes clear. But in the meantime he has done a valuable service in drawing to the attention of a wider public the extent of the bibliographical work already achieved, its nature and its whereabouts. Such information is indispensable for effective research into the many and urgent problems of the sub-continent of Southern Africa.

DOUGLAS VARLEY

Liverpool University
March 1970.

Preface

'South Africa is easily the most thoroughly documented African country south of the Sahara: there exists a vast literature.' These words which have been used to preface an important study[1] on the Transkei, a Southern African territory which is the focus of international attention, also characterise the bibliographical situation.

Although South Africa has always been rich in bibliographical studies, the attention which is now focused on it for political and other reasons, has resulted in a great flood of published material about the country. As a result, some form of bibliographical control has become a pressing necessity, and is the principal reason for the appearance of this text. Books and bibliographies in all fields of knowledge relating to the African scene are in profusion, often filling vital gaps, but no previous evaluation of this material from the bibliographical angle has been attempted up to now.

The book is intended to serve as a companion text to D. H. Borchardt's *Australian Bibliography*,[2] which has been so well received in overseas bibliographical circles. A. J. Walford, editor of the *Guide to Reference Material* has on more than one occasion emphasised the value of regional bibliographies of this kind. The Utopian ideal of achieving world bibliographical coverage, currently and retrospectively, within the covers of a single comprehensive tool, remains elusive. T. Besterman's *World Bibliography of Bibliographies*[3] and of the *Bibliographic*

---

1 CARTER, G. M. *and others. South Africa's Transkei.* London, Heinemann, 1967. p. 189.

2 BORCHARDT., D. H. *Australian Bibliography;* 2nd ed. Melbourne, Cheshire, 1966.

3 BESTERMAN, T. *World Bibliography of Bibliographies;* 4th ed.

5

Index[4] are sufficient proof of how difficult it is to realise this aim.

Progress reports on the bibliographical situation in South Africa have appeared regularly since 1958 in *South African Libraries*, the official organ of the South African Library Association. The present work represents a consolidation of the principal topics and items recorded in these reports.

The majority of the bibliographies mentioned in this book were published in South Africa, but works originating abroad and considered to be of cardinal importance have also been included.

Lausanne, Societas Bibliographica, 1965-1966. 5v. South
Africa: v.1, p. 179-185.
4 Bibliographic Index. New York, Wilson, 1938-.

Acknowledgements

I am grateful to the many librarians throughout South Africa who have over a period of ten years provided information in response to an unending flow of questionnaires.

I am indebted also to the academic staff at Rhodes University who have given me the benefit of their specialised knowledge in evaluating the subject fields pinpointed in this book.

I much appreciate the foreword by Mr. D. H. Varley, University Librarian Harold Cohen Library, Liverpool, who as Lecturer in Bibliography at the University of Cape Town in 1954 aroused my interest in the subject of bibliographical control and who has continued to inspire me ever since.

Contents

1 | Retrospective National Bibliographies

EARLY PRINTED CATALOGUES

Although South Africa has a comparatively small population with a young library profession (the South African Library Association was founded in 1930) and an equally young bibliographical tradition which only came into its own in the twentieth century, there were nevertheless many attempts at bibliography earlier than this, and there are copious instances of libraries which went as far as to publish printed catalogues of their holdings.

Of printed library catalogues recorded by Newenham who has made a bibliographical study of this material,[1] the earliest known appears to be that of the South African Library (1862).[2] This was not however intended to be a national bibliography.

Twenty-four years later in 1886, Fairbridge and Noble compiled a *Catalogue of Books Relating to South Africa*,[3] which marks the first systematic attempt at a bibliography of material about South Africa and especially the Cape of Good Hope, based on the holdings of the South African Library and the private Fairbridge Collection now in the South African Library. Fairbridge's Catalogue lists 600 works but is void of collections of voyages and travels, blue books, parliamentary papers and pamphlets.

---

1   NEWENHAM, E. A. *A Bibliography of Printed Catalogues of the Libraries of South Africa*, 1820-1920. Johannesburg, Public Library, 1967.
2   South African Public Library, Cape Town. *General Catalogue;* comp. by F. Maskew. Cape Town, Solomon, 1862.
3   FAIRBRIDGE, C. A. and NOBLE, J. *Catalogue of Books relating to South Africa*. Cape Town, Richards for Colonial and Indian Exhibition Committee, 1886.

The Catalogue of the Grey Collection of the South African Library[4] by W. H. Bleek appeared some years earlier and deserves mention. Both the Collection and the Compiler of the Catalogue are of great interest. The Grey Collection has been called 'a mirror of Western culture' because of the manner in which its contents span a period from the Dark Ages to the eighteenth century. Not only is the Collection rich in early English printed books, including first and second folio Shakespeare editions, but it is also well-endowed with illuminated mediaeval manuscripts.

The catalogue itself was compiled with characteristic precision by a versatile man, W. H. Bleek, whose life and work have formed the substance of research by O. H. Spohr.[5] It is a basic source for philology as much as for bibliography, as it records many of the earliest attempts by missionaries to record Bantu languages on small and primitive presses. The catechisms and word-books which resulted from these missionary efforts now constitute the incunabula of South African printing history. It was largely due to Sir George Grey, a Governor of the Cape in the nineteenth century, that these mission imprints were gathered together in the first instance.

A work which has proved invaluable in so far as the early period of South African printing is concerned is P. W. Laidler's *Pre-Victorian Products of the Cape Press*.[6] Three supple-

---

4   BLEEK, W. H. I. *The Library of H. E. Sir George Grey, K.C.B.* [*Catalogue*]. London, Trübner, 1858. Vol. 1, Pt. 1. *Philology* : South Africa.

5   A detailed bibliography of Dr. Spohr's writings on Bleek appears in : PAMA, C. ed. *The South African Library: its History, Collections and Librarians, 1818-1968.* Cape Town, Balkema, 1968. p. 62.

6   LAIDLER, P. W. Pre-Victorian Products of the Cape Press, 1796-1837. Johannesburg, South African Library Association, 1935. Additional titles by J. Ross in *South African Libraries*. v.4, 1937, p. 130-133.

ments[7] cover the subsequent period from 1838 to 1858.

MENDELSSOHN'S BIBLIOGRAPHY

As far as retrospective South African bibliography is concerned the greatest landmark of all was to appear in the twentieth century. The publication of Sidney Mendelssohn's *South African Bibliography*[8] in 1910 remains as the chief highlight of retrospective bibliography in South Africa. The two volume *Bibliography* was the culmination of eleven years work.

The personal details of Mendelssohn's life have been fully covered by F. R. Bradlow in several contributions.[9] In view of the importance of Mendelssohn in South African bibliography, a brief resumé of his career is not without interest.

Sidney Mendelssohn was born in Exeter, Devon on 31st December 1860, the elder son of a Rabbi of the Jewish faith. When the Rev. Mendelssohn was appointed Minister to the Jewish Congregation of Kimberley in 1878, Sidney followed not long after. Sidney entered the diamond trade, soon prospered and became a director and later chairman (1900) of the New Bultfontein Mining Company. He was also managing director of the Vaal River Diamond and Exploration Company. Books on Africa fascinated him and by 1899 he started collecting on a huge scale. In 1904 he conceived the idea of com-

7   MANDELBROTE, J. C. *The Cape Press, 1838-1850* (1955); SCHON-FRUCHT, R. M. *The Cape Press, 1851-1855* (1955); HERBST, E. E. *The Cape Press, 1856-1858* (1959). Cape Town, University School of Librarianship.

8   MENDELSSOHN, S. *South African Bibliography*. London, Kegan Paul, 1910. 2v. Reprinted London, Holland Press, 1957 and 1958.

9   BRADLOW, F. R. Sidney Mendelssohn and the Mendelssohn Collection. In: *Jewish Affairs*. v. 20, May 1965, p. 12-17; Sidney Mendelssohn: a Short Biography. In: *Quarterly Bulletin of the South African Library*, v. 22, No. 4, June 1968, p. 104-113.

piling a bibliography which reached fruition in 1910. In 1905 he left Kimberley and went to live in England, after which the monumental bibliography became his major preoccupation. He found time also to write two books, *Jews of Africa* and *Jews of Asia*, which were published posthumously in 1920. Mendelssohn died on 26th September 1917, leaving an estate of £30,000 and a smaller bequest for the building up of his Collection which was bequeathed to the South African Government and since 1922 has been housed in the Library of Parliament.

Mendelssohn's approach to the compilation of his *Bibliography* is of still greater interest. He made every effort, using catalogues of booksellers, reinforced by his personal travels throughout the European Continent, to locate items which he had seen mentioned in the Catalogue of Fairbridge and in Theal's *History of South Africa*.

The *Bibliography* contains about 7000 items and is arranged alphabetically by author or by title when the author is not known. The entries are very full, with full author's name, title, imprint and descriptive annotations which are in themselves unique. It is a work of far greater scope than its title indicates, including as it does South African and foreign periodical articles, Imperial Blue Books, a list of autograph letters in his collection, a list of maps and a chronological and topographical subject index to the titles listed in the bibliography.

The original edition of the *Bibliography* has become a rare item of Africana. 450 copies were printed but the work has since been reprinted twice: in 1957 (500 copies) and in 1968 (350 copies), on both occasions by the Holland Press, London.

Work on the famous *Bibliography* did not cease on publication in 1910. Mendelssohn himself continued to collect, catalogue and annotate books of Africana, so that by the time he died in 1917, he himself had completed six further typescript volumes of new entries. The Library of Parliament to whom the Collection was bequeathed continued to supplement the

Bibliography, but publication of these was later discontinued.

In 1960, forty-three years after Mendelssohn's death a Revision Project was launched at the South African Library with financial support from the National Council for Social Research. An Advisory Committee supervises the Project and the work of revision is undertaken by a full-time and part-time staff headed by the Editor-in-Chief, Dr. A. M. Lewin Robinson, Chief Librarian of the South African Library. A periodic progress report has been issued.

The aim of this Project is to record omissions from, and corrections to, the original Mendelssohn *Bibliography* as well as additional material published up to 1925. At the time of writing, over 34,000 items have already been added to the original Mendelssohn *Bibliography*. and the Revision is far from complete. These items are not only new titles not previously included, but also variant editions, translations and pamphlets. Maps, periodicals, newspapers, manuscripts and pictures are excluded from the Revision Project.

It should be stressed that the end result of this Revision Project will not be a new edition of Mendelssohn's *Bibliography*, but a complementary work which rectifies, and adds to, the original edition, in the form of a 'union catalogue' of holdings: the card entries can be consulted in the South African Library, Cape Town.

In the meantime an interesting by-product has been created as a result of the Revision Project. This is a six monthly *Mendelssohn Revision Project Bulletin* first issued in March 1966. This takes the form of 'Notes and Queries' and contains details of items from the basic catalogue for which research has been necessary and also some problems arising from the work of revision.

On the fiftieth anniversary of Mendelssohn's death, in September 1967, a Symposium on Mendelssohn, his *Bibliography*, the Mendelssohn Collection and the Revision Project was arranged by the Friends of the South African Library. Articles dealing with these subjects appeared in the *Quarterly Bulletin of the South African Library* in September 1967 and June 1968 as part of the anniversary events.

In his address on this occasion, F. R. Bradlow, Chairman of the Friends of the South African Library, dispelled rumours that Mendelssohn himself was not solely responsible for the *Bibliography*, and reminded his audience of the great importance of the work.[10] He quoted Evans Lewin, renowned bibliographer of the Royal Empire Society as saying that the *Bibliography* was unique in so far as colonial bibliographies are concerned, surpassed similar bibliographies of its kind, and made a major contribution to South African culture.

THEAL'S CATALOGUE

In the excitement of appraising Mendelssohn's *Bibliography* one should not overlook the importance of the bibliographical contributions made by George McCall Theal who found fame as a chronicler of South African history. Theal was born in St. John's, New Brunswick, Canada on 11th April 1837 and came to South Africa at the age of 25 in 1861. After successive spells as teacher, journalist and public servant in the Native Affairs Department of the Cape, he was appointed Archivist in 1879 and Colonial Historiographer in 1891. In 1896 he went to Europe and spent seven years in Archives in Holland, London, Paris, Rome and Lisbon. Thereafter he devoted himself to preparing material for publication.

Theal's *Catalogue of Books and Pamphlets*[11] based on the

---

10 BRADLOW, F. R. *Sidney Mendelssohn: a Short Biography.* In: *Quarterly Bulletin of the South African Library*, v. 22, No. 4, June 1968, p. 104-113.

11 THEAL, G. MCC. *Catalogue of Books and Pamphlets relating to Africa South of the Zambesi.* Cape Town, *Cape Times*, 1912. Reprinted Cape Town, Struik, 1963.

works in his own Collection, but also on works in the South African Library and in the British Museum, is of greatest interest for its critical annotations, chiefly from the point of view of an archivist-librarian. Like Mendelssohn's *Bibliography*, Theal's *Catalogue* is an author bibliography, but it is not nearly as comprehensive and no attempt has ever been made to supplement it. The *Catalogue* has however been reprinted by C. Struik to meet the continual demand for it, and it remains of great interest to Africana collectors.

CATALOGUES OF THE ROYAL EMPIRE SOCIETY

One of the most important publications in retrospective South African bibliography between the first and second World Wars of the twentieth century was the *Subject Catalogue of the Royal Empire Society*.[12] The first volume of this Catalogue, although it deals also with many territories other than South Africa, remains a cardinal source of bibliographical information on South African affairs, and all the more so in the absence of a national bibliography for this period. A further volume[13] published in 1961 was devoted entirely to biography and included over 700 South African items.

The period between the two World Wars was otherwise undistinguished in the South African bibliographical scene. National bibliography was virtually non-existent until the State Library began to publish annual lists of material received under legal deposit in 1936.[14] It was in fact left to individual

---

12 ROYAL EMPIRE SOCIETY. Subject Catalogue of the Library by P. Evans Lewin. v.1: British Empire generally and Africa. London, The Society, 1930.

13 Royal Commonwealth Society. *Biography Catalogue of the Library*, by D. H. Simpson. London, The Society, 1961.

14 State Library, Pretoria. Accession Lists. Monthly: 1933-1959. Annual Cumulations: 1938-1959.

B

enterprise to revive the concept of a comprehensive national bibliography.

CONTRIBUTION OF N. S. COETZEE

In 1939 Nico S. Coetzee published the *South African Catalogue of Books*[15] covering the period 1900-1939 in some 4000-5000 entries. By 1950 the work had grown to two volumes and passed through four editions. The Compiler's aim was to include all books published in South Africa in English, Afrikaans and African languages, with the exception of government publications and mission presses. Full author, title, and imprint details were included, and price as well. The work was marred by reproduction on poor paper, unsatisfactory typing and numerous omissions and inaccuracies which severely limited its use. It nevertheless remains useful as the only tool of its kind in a bleak period of South African bibliography. The Catalogue died completely with the first volume covering letters A-K of a projected fifth edition covering the years 1900-54 and published in 1956.

The serious gap in the South African bibliographical record between the commencement of the current national bibliographies in 1958/59 and the terminal date of the Mendelssohn Revision Project (1925) is at last receiving attention at national level.

The State Library, Pretoria, is making good progress with the compilation of a retrospective bibliography of the years 1926-1958. As an essential preliminary, the Library is making every effort to locate original or photo-reproduced copies of works missing from its Copyright Collection.

---

15   COETZEE, N. S. *South African Catalogue of Books.* 1st ed. 1900–1939 published 1941; 2nd ed. 1900-1942 published 1943; 3rd ed. 1900-1947 published 1948; 4th ed. 1900-1950 published 1950; 5th ed. 1900-1954 (Vol. 1 only) published 1956.

BIBLIOGRAPHIES OF PROFESSOR P. J. NIENABER

The work of Professor P. J. Nienaber represents another solo and unique effort in retrospective South African bibliography. Professor Nienaber's work has taken the form of systematic documentation of all books in the Afrikaans language known to exist from 1861 to the present time.[16] As in the case of Mendelssohn, this is an instance of a collector, intensely interested in a subject, in Nienaber's case the subject being Afrikaans literature of which he is a Professor at the University of the Witwatersrand, and setting about the task of cataloguing all the books in his chosen field.

Nienaber has come remarkably close to recording every single work published in Afrikaans, and the six volumes published to date give full author, title and subject lists, as well as lists of pseudonyms and directories of publishers. In the absence of a formal national retrospective bibliography, Nienaber's work is invaluable for Afrikaans language bibliography.

It is regrettable that no similar record exists for the English language book in South Africa, but attention is drawn later in this text to helpful works which assist in filling the gap in the writer's discussion of subject bibliographies.

ROLE OF DR. O. H. SPOHR

Credit should be given to Dr. O. H. Spohr for his individual efforts to produce a comprehensive record of German language publications on South Africa and South West Africa.[17] Dr. Spohr is South Africa's foremost specialist on German Afri-

---

16 NIENABER, P. J. *Bibliografie van Afrikaanse Boeke.* Johannesburg. The Author, 1943-1967. 6v.

17 SPOHR, O. H. *German Africana: German Publications on South and South West Africa.* Pretoria, State Library, 1968. (State Library. Bibliographies, No. 14).

cana, and his author bibliography of 3423 items is the most comprehensive record of its kind, far surpassing the Southern African content in the list[18] of Bridgman and Clarke at the Hoover Institution, and representing as it does a consolidation of all previous German Africana bibliographies published in South Africa. The main author list is complemented by a subject index, and an additional useful feature of the bibliography is the way in which the Compiler has given locations of works cited. Dr. Spohr's bibliography will almost certainly come to be regarded as the definitive bibliography in its field.

Handicapped by the lack of a comprehensive national bibliography for the period prior to 1959, one is bound to turn to selective bibliographies issued at various times, all of which make a contribution towards filling the gap in the bibliographical record.

One such bibliography which deserves special mention is *South Africa in Print*,[19] issued in conjunction with a national exhibition to mark the van Riebeeck Tercentenary in 1952 and forming an excellent select list of Africana. This important bibliography is arranged in broad subject groups e.g. South African English literature, language and literature of African peoples, development of South African printing. There are full annotations for most entries, and each section is prefaced by a good introduction. Another example is the exhibition catalogue compiled for the Union Festival in 1960,[20] very selective in its choice of material and unfortunately not annotated.

---

18   BRIDGMAN, J. and CLARKE, D. E. *German Africa: a Select Annotated Bibliography*. Stanford, Hoover Institution, 1965.

19   Van Riebeeck Festival, 1952. *South Africa in Print: Catalogue of an Exhibition of Books, Atlases and Maps held in the South African Library, Cape Town*, March-April 1952. Cape Town, Book Exhibition Committee, 1952.

20   UNION FESTIVAL, 1960. *The Book in South Africa: Exhibition of South African Publications*, 9-31 May 1960. Bloemfontein, Union Festival Committee, 1960.

2 | Current National Bibliographies

There are several unusual features, which characterise the national bibliographical situation in South Africa. One is the existence of two national libraries,* another is the high incidence of legal deposit libraries entitled to receive material published in South Africa.

Fortunately the functions of the two national libraries are now clearly demarcated, the State Library, Pretoria, serving primarily as a national bibliographical and lending service, and the South African Library, Cape Town, as a national reference library. Both libraries publish national bibliographies.

THE STATE LIBRARY, PRETORIA

From 1933 to 1958, the State Library published monthly mimeographed lists of publications received under copyright legislation, i.e. the Patents, Designs and Trade Marks Act 9 of 1916. These monthly lists were cumulated annually and arranged alphabetically by author, giving full information for author, title, imprint, collation, series and occasionally price. No attempt was made at annotation. Government publications (central and provincial) were included. Mention has already been made in Chapter One of the State Library's project aimed at consolidating this period in the form of a single retrospective bibliography which will actually commence with the year 1926 so as to fill the gap between the terminal date of the Mendelssohn Revision Project (1925) and the commencement of the *South African National Bibliography* in 1959.

In 1959, the State Library launched a fully fledged current cumulative national bibliography, quarterly in frequency with

---

*Since this chapter was written the South African Library for the Blind, Grahamstown, has been declared a third national library.

annual cumulations. Unlike its alphabetically arranged fore-
runner, *S.A.N.B.* (as the *South African National Bibliography*
is generally abbreviated) is arranged broadly in Dewey Decimal
Classification order, the entries in each broad group being sub-
arranged alphabetically by author. Full descriptive cataloguing is given, as well as the specific classification number
according to the seventeenth edition of the Dewey Decimal
Classification, and the price.

The scope of the *S.A.N.B.* is broad and includes official
publications, sheet music, children's and school books, novels,
books in Bantu languages and new periodicals (listed alphabetically). Additional information includes book production
and translation statistics, and authors writing under pseudonyms are conveniently listed in a separate appendix, as an
additional finding device over and above the entries for
pseudonymous works within the bibliography itself. The classified arrangement is complemented by a full author/title index,
which also gives series and subjects of biographical and critical
works. Since January 1968 the *S.A.N.B.* has been reproduced
by mechanised methods. The first cumulative issue for 1959 to
1967 is in preparation.

Arising out of the *S.A.N.B.* a great step forward bibliographically was taken in January 1967 when the State Library
introduced a card service.

The *S.A.N.B.* Card Service provides weekly announcements
of new South African publications received under the provi-
sions of the Copyright Act. A full title description and the
Dewey Decimal Classification number is provided for each
publication on a standard catalogue card. Other information
provided includes notification of new and ceased periodicals,
names and addresses of publishers not previously listed in the
S.A.N.B., and entries for reprints received in terms of an agree-
ment with the South African Publishers' Association. The
Card Service prides itself on the speed of its appearance;

entries appear on cards within seven days of the receipt of the relevant item at the State Library, and cards are despatched at weekly intervals. The subscription for 1968 was Twenty-six Rands for the first set of cards.

Of the eighty subscribers as at 1968, twenty are South African libraries while eight are libraries abroad, including two sets which are supplied to the Library of Congress in Washington for the Shared Cataloguing Programme. The majority of subscribers are booksellers.

In response to a motion passed at the 1966 South African Library Association's Annual Conference, attention is now being given by the State Library to the possibility of employing the card service to provide a centralised cataloguing service for South African publications. However, the poor national response to the Card Service is a deterrent to further progress in this regard.

THE SOUTH AFRICAN LIBRARY, CAPE TOWN

National bibliography at the other national library, viz. the South African Library may be said to have commenced in September 1946 when the *Quarterly Bulletin of the South African Library* first appeared, and contained from the very first issue until 1958 a classified bibliography of material relating to South Africa. In 1958 this Bibliography, which was based on the legal deposit material received in the Africana Department of the South African Library, emerged as a separate publication under the title: *Africana Nova*, the first issue appearing in September of that year.

Africana Nova is a classified bibliography of books currently published in and about South Africa, and unlike the *South African National Bibliography* is not limited to works bearing South African imprints. This is the cardinal difference in scope between the two national bibliographies, but there are other differences as well. For example, whereas *S.A.N.B.* is classified according to the Dewey Decimal Classification, *Africana Nova* is arranged according to the Universal Decimal Classification. Also, in contrast to the *S.A.N.B.*, the quarterly issues of *Africana Nova* are not cumulated, but a cumulative author/title index is included in the final issue for each year and serves to cumulate the year's entries. Since March 1962 a list of new official publications has been included.

It remains to be seen how long the country can continue to have two national bibliographies which duplicate each other to such a large extent.*

OTHER LEGAL DEPOSIT LIBRARIES

Mention has been made earlier in this Chapter of the existence of several libraries entitled to receive material under legal deposit. The privilege of legal deposit has been operative since Act 9 of 1916 was promulgated. Besides the State Library and the South African Library, other legal deposit libraries are the Natal Society Library in Pietermaritzburg, the Bloemfontein Public Library, and the Library of Parliament (since 1922). It is interesting to note that the British Museum Library was also awarded legal deposit privilege in the Act. Although the Act has since been replaced by Copyright Act 63 of 1965, there are no changes in so far as the South African legal deposit libraries are concerned, but the British Museum's privilege was deleted.

The multiplicity of these legal deposit libraries, was one of the reasons which prompted Mr. J. Willemse to make the study of the legal deposit privilege the theme of his dissertation for the Master's Degree in Library Science.[1] This has since

---

1   WILLEMSE, J. 'Die Pligeksemplaar, Voorreg met besondere Verwysing na Suid-Afrika'. M.A. (Library Science) Dissertation, University of Pretoria, 1962.
*   *Africana Nova* ceased publication in December 1969.

been re-published in the periodical *Mousaion*[2] and so made available to a wide audience.

In so far as national bibliography is concerned, the Bloemfontein Public Library and the Natal Society Library issue monthly lists of accessions, which appear so promptly and consequently so far ahead of the two national bibliographies, that they have definite value as part of the national bibliographical apparatus. Both lists take the form of author bibliographies, but the entries themselves are not as full as those in the two national bibliographies.

THE BOOK TRADE

The contribution of the book trade towards current national bibliography should not be overlooked. In South Africa one firm in particular has built up an enviable reputation in this regard. C. Struik of Cape Town has issued a good many bibliographies in recent years. None claims to be exhaustive, but they remain extremely useful in the absence of more formal lists and especially in the absence of a national 'books-in-print' and 'book auction' record. Among the bibliographies issued by the firm are: *Catalogue of Books (English) published in Southern Africa Still in Print* (1966-68); and *Katalogus van Boeke in Afrikaans Verkrygbaar* (1968). The same firm has also published lists of South African imprints up to 1900, as well as lists of English and Afrikaans South African novels, but the most important list issued at regular intervals since 1956 is the firm's catalogue of Africana offered for sale. This series of catalogues, of which sixty-six had been issued by February 1969 go a long way towards providing antiquarian book price information for works of Africana.

---

2   WILLEMSE, J. 'The Legal Deposit Privilege with Special Reference to South Africa.' In: *Mousaion*. Nos. 68-69. 1963.

There are not many other firms so bibliographically active in South Africa, but F. Thorold (Johannesburg), G. Bakker (Johannesburg) and G. Clarke (Cape Town) have issued useful catalogues from time to time. The catalogues of F. Kitch (Cape Town) were a valuable source of information between the two World Wars.

3 | Subject Bibliographies

The basic tool for establishing whether or not a bibliography exists on a South African subject is the South African Library's *Bibliography of African Bibliographies*.[1] This work first appeared in 1942, a second edition was published in 1948, a third in 1955 and a fourth edition in 1961. At the time of writing (1969) no new edition has appeared, but is promised for the near future.

Until such time as a revision appears, the only way of determining whether a subject has been covered since November 1960 which is the terminal date of entries in the 1961 edition, is to consult the national bibliographies or R. Musiker's Bibliographical progress reports in *South African Libraries*[2] and in the *South African Library Association Newsletter*.[3] The two consolidated lists of bibliographies compiled for Librarianship Diploma purposes at the University of Cape Town[4] and Witwatersrand University[5] are also useful, but

1 South African Library, Cape Town. *A Bibliography of African Bibliographies covering Territories South of the Sahara*. Cape Town, South African Library, 1942-.
2 MUSIKER, R. 'Bibliographical Progress in South Africa.' 1961/63. In: *South African Libraries*, v.31, No. 2, Oct. 1963, p. 49-58; 1963/64 In: *South African Libraries*, v.33, No. 2, Oct. 1965, p. 55-64; 1965-66 In: *South African Libraries*, v.35, No. 2, Oct. 1967, p. 57-64; 1967/68 In: *South African Libraries*, v.37, No. 1, Jul. 1969, p. 13-19.
3 MUSIKER, R. 'Bibliographical Progress.' In: *South African Library Association Newsletter*, v. 17, No. 11, May 1966; v. 18, No. 11, May 1967; v. 19, No. 2, Aug. 1967; v. 19, No. 11, May 1968; v. 20, No. 11, May 1969; v. 21, No. 3, Sept. 1969.
4 University of Cape Town. School of Librarianship. Bibliographical Series: Consolidated List, 1941-1966. Cape Town, University of Cape Town Libraries, 1966.
5 University of the Witwatersrand. Department of Bibliography, Librarianship and Typography. Bibliographies . . . a List of

these are in alphabetical order and have no subject arrangement.

The South African entries in the *Bibliography of African Bibliographies*[6] published by the Cambridge African Studies Centre in 1967 and in the universally known *World Bibliography of Bibliographies*[7] by Theodore Besterman (fourth edition, 1965-66) are uneven and very inadequate in their coverage of South Africa. They are also regrettably full of errors, and far more out of date than the imprints on their title-pages would lead one to believe.

The South African Library's *Bibliography of African Bibliographies* (fourth edition, 1961) listed over 1340 entries, arranged according to the Universal Decimal Classification, and emphasising specific subjects throughout. It is beyond the scope of the present work to recapitulate all of them, especially as many new items have been published since then. Instead it is the writer's aim to select the more important subject areas and to pinpoint the basic bibliographies in each field as at 1969. In making this selection emphasis is laid on more recent bibliographies.

Neither the Cambridge nor the South African Library's *Bibliography of African Bibliographies* makes any attempt to annotate or evaluate South African bibliographies. They do not answer the question: Which is the basic, best or most useful bibliography on a particular subject? and it is hoped that the present work will fill a gap in this respect.

Many of the subject bibliographies mentioned in this Chap-

Items Currently Available. Johannesburg, The Department, 1968.
6   GARLING, A. *A Bibliography of African Bibliographies.* Cambridge, African Studies Centre, 1967.
7   BESTERMAN, T. *World Bibliography of Bibliographies;* 4th ed. Lausanne, Societas Bibliographica, 1965-1966. 5 v. v. 1, p. 179-185.

ter are the work of students, and were compiled in partial ful-
filment of the requirements for the post-graduate Diplomas in
Librarianship at South African universities. The student bibliographies vary in quality. Some have not been published while
others, although not entirely satisfactory, are nevertheless the
only sources in a particular field and are mentioned for this
reason. The quality or standard of a particular bibliography has
not however been used as a criterion in the selection of the
item for inclusion in this Chapter.

For the convenience of librarians using this book, the subjects are arranged in broad Dewey Decimal Classification
sequence. All subjects will be found listed alphabetically in
the index to this book.

020 LIBRARIANSHIP

Le Sueur's *Bibliographic Guide to South African Librarianship*[8] is a massive basic guide to the literature of South
African librarianship prior to 1953. This three-volume work
is arranged according to the Dewey Decimal Classification
and complemented by relative and author indices, yet it
remains an awkward tool to use largely because of the poor
typographical layout. The work is now considerably out-
of-date, but it remains useful as a starting point in a search.
A much briefer bibliography[9] by P. Freer and others had
been published as long ago as 1937.

Specific fields in South African librarianship have been
covered to some extent by several theses. Theo Friis' *The*

---

8   LE SUEUR, A. G. *Bibliographic Guide to South African Librarianship*. Cape Town, University School of Librarianship, 1954.
3v.

9   FREER, P. AND OTHERS. 'Bibliography of South African Libraries and Librarianship.' In: Report of Interdepartmental Committee on Libraries of the Union of South Africa. Pretoria,
Government Printer, 1937. p. 26-35.

Public Library in South Africa[10] *and* R. Musiker's *Special Libraries*[11] both have considerable bibliographies on South African public and special libraries respectively. A comprehensive bibliography on *South African Special Libraries and Information Services*[12] was compiled by P. Lor at Stellenbosch University in 1967, and another [13] by M. Strydom on the university library in South Africa also at Stellenbosch University in the same year, and one[14] by W. M. Vermeulen on *School Libraries in South Africa*. D. D. Murtagh's bibliography on *Education for Librarianship in Africa*[15] is the most comprehensive source on this subject. Two comprehensive lists of recommended books for children and school libraries respectively have been compiled fairly recently; the former[16] by Lydia Pienaar for the Cape Town City Libraries

---

10   FRIIS, T. *The Public Library in South Africa: an Evaluative Study*. Cape Town, Afrikaanse Pers, 1962; *and* London, Deutsch, 1962. p. 342-349.

11   MUSIKER, R. 'Special Libraries: a General Survey with Special Reference to South Africa.' M.A. (Library Science) Dissertation, University of Pretoria, 1968. Published by Scarecrow Press, Metuchen (N.J.), 1970.

12   LOR, P. J. 'Special Libraries and Information Services in South Africa: Bibliography.' Stellenbosch, University, Department of Librarianship, 1967. Unpublished.

13   STRYDOM, M. 'Bibliografie van Universiteits-en Universiteitskollege-biblioteke in Suid-Afrika.' Stellenbosch, University, Department of Librarianship, 1967. Unpublished.

14   VERMEULEN, W. M. *School Libraries in South Africa, 1920-1963: a Select Bibliography*. Cape Town, University School of Librarianship, 1965.

15   MURTAGH, D. D. *Education for Librarianship in Africa: a Bibliography*. Johannesburg, University of the Witwatersrand, 1968.

16   PIENAAR, L. *Basic Children's Books: a List for a South African Library*. Cape Town, City Libraries, 1966. Supplement 1967.

and the latter[17] by the Transvaal Education Department Library Service.

100 PHILOSOPHY

H. G. Dawe's *Philosophy in South Africa, 1950-1962*,[18] appears to be the only major recent bibliography on this subject.

130 PSYCHOLOGY

Except for an early contribution[19] by P. Skawran, which covers the period to 1933, there is no comprehensive bibliography on this subject in South African context. There are however, several fine bibliographical studies dealing with specific subjects in psychology.

L. E. Andor's bibliography on the *Aptitudes and Abilities of the Non-White Peoples in South Africa*[20] is a comprehensive, well-annotated contribution on this subject. Another is N. Swanevelder's *Intelligence*[21] and M. Rosengarten's bibliography on *Intelligence Tests in Non-Europeans*.[22]

---

17 Transvaal (Province). *Education Department. Library Service. Book Guide; cumulative issue, 1961-1966.* Pretoria, The Department, 1968.

18 DAWE, H. G. A. *Philosophy in South Africa, 1950-1962: a Bibliography.* Cape Town, University, School of Librarianship, 1964.

19 SKAWRAN, P. 'South African Psychological Literature.' In: *South African Journal of Psychology and Education.* v.1, No. 2, 1933, p. 67-86.

20 ANDOR, L. E. *Aptitudes and Abilities of the Black Man in Sub-Saharan Africa, 1784-1963.* Johannesburg, National Institute for Personnel Research, 1966.

21 SWANEVELDER, N. *Intelligence: a Bibliography of South African Literature on Intelligence, 1940-1967.* Stellenbosch, University Department of Librarianship, 1967.

22 ROSENGARTEN, M. 'Intelligence Tests on Non-Europeans in South Africa.' Cape Town, University, School of Librarianship, 1959. Unpublished.

200 RELIGION

Most of the bibliographical literature falls within the scope of mission topics. Du Plessis' standard work on the *History of Christian Missions in South Africa*[23] has a long and basic bibliography. Brownlee's bibliography[24] on South African missionaries also covered a wide field, while P. J. Frost's bibliography[25] was limited to Natal. Since then several fairly comprehensive bibliographies on specific denominations have been published: C. E. P. Turnbull has dealt with the missionaries of the Dutch Reformed Church up to 1910,[26] and M. J. Cowie has covered the London Missionary Society in South Africa.[27] A bibliography[28] by C. Tait on the History of the Presbyterian Church in South Africa is in preparation.

300 SOCIOLOGY

Four specific themes which have been well covered biblio-

23　DU PLESSIS, J. *History of Christian Missions in South Africa.* London, Longmans, 1911, p. 446-479. Reprinted, Cape Town, Struik, 1965, p. 446-479.

24　BROWNLEE, M. *The Lives and Work of South African Missionaries: a bibliography.* Cape Town, University, School of Librarianship, 1952.

25　FROST, P. J. *A Bibliography of Missions and Missionaries in Natal.* Cape Town, University, School of Librarianship, 1965.

26　TURNBULL, C. E. P. *The Work of the Missionaries of Die Nederduitse Gereformeerde Kerk van Suid-Afrika up to the year 1910.* Johannesburg, University of the Witwatersrand, Department of Bibliography, Librarianship and Typography, 1965.

27　COWIE, M. J. *The London Missionary Society in South Africa: a Bibliography.* Cape Town. University, School of Librarianship, 1967.

28　TAIT, C. *History of the Presbyterian Church in South Africa: a Bibliography.* In Preparation at University of the Witwatersrand, Department of Bibliography, Librarianship and Typography.

graphically very recently are juvenile delinquency[29] by M. M. Boshoff, the status of women in South Africa[30] by R. Dubow, care of the aged[31] by O. M. Young, and rehabilitation of the physically handicapped[32] by B. J. Gosling.

310 STATISTICS

A two volume bibliographical guide to statistical sources and publications[33] was published in 1962 by the University of South Africa's Bureau of Market Research.

320 POLITICS AND RACE RELATIONS

The political scene in recent years has been a subject of greater interest than possibly any other. As a result bibliographies are as numerous as texts. The difficulty in this field is to maintain objectivity and impartiality, and few bibliographies succeed entirely in this respect. Among the most comprehensive bibliographies are those which appear annually in the *Survey of Race Relations*[34] compiled by the South African Institute for Race Relations. Although they were not published in South Africa, the very full critically

---

29　BOSHOFF, M. M. *Juvenile Delinquency in South Africa.* Cape Town, University, School of Librarianship, 1965.

30　DUBOW, R. *Status of Women in South Africa: a Select Bibliography.* Cape Town, University, School of Librarianship, 1965.

31　YOUNG, O. M. *Care of the Aged in South Africa, 1822-1963: a Select Bibliography.* Cape Town, University, School of Librarianship, 1964.

32　GOSLING, B. J. *Rehabilitation of the Physically Handicapped in South Africa, 1950-1960.* Cape Town, University, School of Librarianship, 1965.

33　GEERTSEMA, G. *Guide to Statistical Sources in the Republic of South Africa.* Pretoria, University of South Africa, Bureau of Market Research, 1962. 2v.

34　South African Institute of Race Relations. *Survey of Race Relations in South Africa.* Johannesburg, The Institute, 1954-

C

annotated bibliographies[35] appended to Professor Gwendolen Carter's books on South Africa are among the best in this field. G. M. M. Hodge's Bibliography[36] covers the key period 1933-1939.

The Indian Peoples in South Africa have been covered in several bibliographies,[37] as have the Coloured Peoples[38] and the Bantu.[39]

330 ECONOMICS

D. Hobart Houghton's standard work on *The South African*

35　CARTER, G. M. *The Politics of Inequality: South Africa since 1948;* 2nd ed. London, Thames & Hudson, 1959, p. 497-524; CARTER, G. M. *Five African States.* London, Pall Mall, 1964. Includes South Africa. Bibl. p. 607-616.

36　HODGE, G. M. M. *South African Politics, 1933-1939.* Cape Town, University, School of Librarianship, 1965.

37　South Africa (Republic). National Bureau of Educational and Social Research. Bibliography on the Indians in South Africa. Pretoria, Government Printer [1964] (Information Series No. 7).
MORRIS, G. R. *A Bibliography of the Indian Question in South Africa.* Cape Town, University, School of Librarianship, 1950; CURRIE, J. C. *A Bibliography of Material Published during the Period 1946-56 on the Indian Question in South Africa.* Cape Town, University, School of Librarianship, 1959.

38　South Africa (Union). *Department of Coloured Affairs. General Bibliography: the Coloured People of South Africa.* Cape Town, The Department, 1960; JACOBSON, E. *The Cape Coloured: a Bibliography.* Cape Town, University School of Librarianship, 1950; CANIN, C. The Cape Coloured People, 1945 to 1950: a Bibliography. Cape Town, University School of Librarianship, 1959. Not published; MANUEL, G. *The Coloured People: a Bibliography.* Cape Town, University, School of Librarianship, 1950.

39　VILJOEN, R. A. *Bibliography on the Bantu in the Republic of South Africa.* Pretoria. National Bureau of Educational and Social Research, 1966. (Information Series, No. 12.)

Economy[40] is equipped with a fine bibliography on the sub-ject and has the advantage of being relatively up-to-date, and much more so than the 1959 bibliography by the Scienti-fic Council for Africa.[41]

340 LAW

The basic bibliography of Roman and Roman Dutch legal literature in South Africa is A. A. Roberts' *South African Legal Bibliography*,[42] which is really much more than its name implies. Not only does the work offer a wealth of biographical information on authors and the South African judiciary, but the very full annotations, which include loca-tions of legal works held in South Africa, make this one of the country's truly great bibliographical landmarks. Pub-lished in 1942, the work is now out-of-date to some extent, but a revised edition by Professor B. Beinart of the Depart-ment of Law at the University of Cape Town is in prepara-tion. A briefer bibliography of the most important items published since 1910 is included in Hahlo and Kahn, *South Africa: the Development of its Laws and Constitution*.[43] Current bibliographical coverage of law is provided by the

---

40 HOUGHTON, D. H. *The South African Economy;* 2nd ed. Cape Town, Oxford University Press, 1967. p. 265-272.

41 Scientific Council for Africa South of the Sahara. *Inventory of Economic Studies concerning Africa South of the Sahara: an Annotated Reading List.* London, Commission for Technical Co-operation in Africa South of the Sahara, 1959. (Publica-tion No. 30.)

42 ROBERTS, A. A. *South African Legal Bibliography: being a Bio-Bibliographical Survey and Law-Finder of the Roman and Roman-Dutch Legal Literature in South Africa.* Pretoria, Wallach, 1942.

43 HAHLO, H. R. and KAHN, E. *South Africa: the Development of its Laws and Constitution.* Cape Town, Juta, 1960, p. 815-829.

Annual Survey of South African Law[44] which includes a checklist of legal publications. Although they were not published in South Africa, mention should be made of two important bibliographies of South African law compiled by specialists in their fields, and covering over 200 items between them. A. J. Kerr's bibliography[45] deals with Bantu Law, while P. Van Warmelo's contribution[46] covers modern South African Law. B. Kuper's *Bibliography of Native Law* [46a] covers the years 1941-1961, and consists of 119 items relating to African customary tribal law.

355 MILITARY HISTORY

M. K. Vrdoljak has compiled a bibliography[47] on the history of South African regiments, while the Johannesburg Public Library's *Catalogue of British Regimental Histories*[48] is especially useful because of the copious notes on the service of these regiments in South Africa.

---

44 *Annual Survey of South African Law.* Cape Town, Juta, 1948-.

45 KERR, A. J. *Bantu Law in the Republic of South Africa.* Brussels, Institut de Sociologie, 1964. (Bibliographical Introduction to Legal History and Ethnology, E.31).

46 VAN WARMELO, P. *Afrique du Sud: Droit Moderne,* Brussels, Institut de Sociologie, 1963. (Bibliographical Introduction to Legal History and Ethnology, E.32).

46a KUPER, B. *A Bibliography of Native Law in South Africa, 1941-1961.* Johannesburg, University of the Witwatersrand, Department of Librarianship, 1962. Reprinted in: *African Studies,* v.23, Nos. 3/4, 1964, p. 155-165.

47 VRDOLJAK, M. K. *The History of South African Regiments: a Select Bibliography.* Cape Town, University, School of Librarianship, 1959.

48 Johannesburg Public Library. Catalogue of British Regimental Histories with Notes on their Service in South Africa. Johannesburg, The Library, 1953.

370 EDUCATION

The bibliographies by G. Levy and J. M. Marcus on *European Education in South Africa*[49] cover the period 1922 to 1955 and serve to up-date the basic bibliography for 1652 to 1922 given in E. G. Malherbe's basic text on the history of education in South Africa.[50] The period since 1946 is covered to some extent in the bibliographies appended to several books surveying education in South Africa which have appeared in recent years, for example: *Education in South Africa*[51] by A. L. Behr and R. G. MacMillan.

The subject of Bantu education in the decade 1949-1959 has been dealt with in a bibliography[52] compiled by Lydia Potgieter. Likewise, the education of the Coloured peoples has been covered by C. Taylor's bibliography.[53] E. R. Shandling has compiled a bibliography[54] on vocational education in South Africa, 1920-1965.

---

49 LEVY, G. *European Education in South Africa, 1922-1946: a Select Bibliography*. Cape Town, University, School of Librarianship, 1949; MARCUS, J. M. *European Education in South Africa, 1946-1955: a Select Bibliography*. Cape Town, University, School of Librarianship, 1959.

50 MALHERBE, E. G. *Education in South Africa, 1652-1922*. Cape Town, Juta, 1925. p. 483-504.

51 BEHR, A. L. and MACMILLAN, R. G. *Education in South Africa*. Pretoria, Van Schaik, 1966.

52 POTGIETER, L. *A Bibliography of Bantu Education in the Union of South Africa, 1949-1959*. Cape Town, University, School of Librarianship, 1965.

53 TAYLOR, C. J. *Coloured Education*. Cape Town, University, School of Librarianship, 1966.

54 SHANDLING, E. R. *Vocational Guidance in South Africa, 1920-1965*. Cape Town, University, School of Librarianship, 1967.

383 PHILATELY

Two bibliographies by M. D. M. Begley[55] and D. R. Nott[56] cover South African philately of the pre-Union (1910) and post-Union periods respectively.

387 TRANSPORTATION

E. Joubert has covered[57] South African road transportation in the nineteenth century, while M. V. Buckland has done likewise[58] for South African railways in the period prior to 1910.

490 BANTU LANGUAGES

Two earlier catalogues although intended primarily as guides to special collections on African languages are nevertheless very useful for bibliographical purposes. These are A. H. Smith's *Catalogue of Bantu, Khoisan and Malagasy in the Strange Collection of Africana, Johannesburg Public Library*,[59] which was published in 1942 and consisted of 1671 entries; and D. Rossouw's *Catalogue of African Languages, 1858-1900 in the Grey Collection, South African*

---

55 BEGLEY, M. D. M. A Bibliography of South African Philately: Pre-Union Period. Cape Town, University, School of Librarianship, 1954. Unpublished.

56 NOTT, D. R. A Bibliography of South African Philately: Post-Union Period. Cape Town, University, School of Librarianship, 1954. Unpublished.

57 JOUBERT, E. *Road Transportation in South Africa in the 19th Century*: Bibliography. Cape Town, University, School of Librarianship, 1955.

58 BUCKLAND, M. V. *South African Railways before 1910: a Bibliography*. Cape Town, University, School of Librarianship, 1964.

59 SMITH, A. H. *Catalogue of Bantu, Khoisan and Malagasy in the Strange Collection of Africana*. Johannesburg, Public Library, 1942.

Library, Cape Town,[60] published in 1947 and consisting of 379 entries. More recently (1959-1963) the South African Government's Department of Bantu Education published a set of six volumes devoted to the bibliography of the Bantu languages in the Republic of South Africa.[61]

550 GEOLOGY

M. Wilman's bibliography[62] is the most important and comprehensive for the early period. A bibliography of South African geology[63] has been published annually since 1957. This work supplements the basic *Bibliography of South African Geology*[64] compiled by A. L. Hall for the period up to 1935.

Another basic work in this field *Mineral Resources of the Union of South Africa*[65] is well provided with bibliographies at the end of most chapters.

---

60 ROSSOUW, D. E. *Catalogue of African Languages, 1858-1900 in the Grey Collection of the South African Library, Cape Town.* Cape Town, University, School of Librarianship, 1947.

61 South Africa (Republic). *Department of Bantu Education. Bibliography of the Bantu Languages in the Republic of South Africa.* Pretoria, The Department, 1959-1963. 6v.

62 WILMAN, M. 'Catalogue of Printed Books, Papers and Maps relating to the Geology and Mineralogy of South Africa to 1904.' In: *South African Philosophical Society. Transactions.* v.15, No. 5, 1905, p. 283-467.

63 South Africa (Republic). Geological Survey. *Bibliography and Subject Index of South African Geology.* Pretoria, The Survey, 1957-.
South Africa (Republic). Geological Survey. Abstracts of Geological Literature Received . . . Part 1: Southern Africa.

64 HALL, A. L. *Bibliography of South African Geology to 1935.* Pretoria, Government Printer, 1922-1939. 6v.

65 South Africa (Union). Geological Survey. *The Mineral Resources of the Union of South Africa;* 4th ed. Pretoria, Government Printer, 1959.

Currently, a catalogue of the publications of the Geological Survey is issued as an addendum to the Government's Department of Mines *Quarterly Information Circular*.

The University of Natal, Pietermaritzburg, issued a mimeographed *Bibliography of Geomorphological Literature*,[66] revised to October 1962.

551 METEOROLOGY

J. G. Gamble's Catalogue[67] is basic to this section. The Government's Weather Bureau has compiled a multi-volume *Bibliography of Regional Meteorological Literature*.[68] Volume three published in 1966 covers the Antarctica (1739-1957), an area of interest to a wide audience.

560 PALAEONTOLOGY

R. Musiker's *The Australopithecinae*[69] is an example of a specialised bibliography in this field. It has been supplemented by A. Meyer.[70]

---

66 University of Natal. *Bibliography of Geomorphological Literature*. Pietermaritzburg, The University, 1962.

67 GAMBLE, J. G. 'Catalogue of Printed Books and Papers Relating to South Africa . . . Climate and Meteorology.' In: *South African Philosophical Society. Transactions*. v.3, 1881-1883, p. 151-196.

68 South Africa (Union). *Weather Bureau. Bibliography of Regional Meteorological Literature*. Pretoria, Government Printer, 1950-.

69 MUSIKER, R. *The Australopithecinae: a Bibliography*. Cape Town, University, School of Librarianship, 1955. Reprinted 1969.

70 MEYER, A. *Hominids of the Lower and Middle Pleistocene: the Australopithecinae and Homo Habilis*. Johannesburg, University of the Witwatersrand, Department of Bibliography, Librarianship and Typography, 1968.

571 ARCHAEOLOGY

The fullest and best current bibliographical survey of South African archaeology is to be found in the Cowa Series of the Council for Old World Archaeology. The triennial Survey for 1965/1968[71] was compiled by H. J. Deacon and covered no less than 215 items, all annotated. This is an excellent bibliographical survey of a scientific discipline and one which could serve as a model for other subject bibliographies. S. E. Holm's *Bibliography of South African Pre- and Proto-Historic Archaeology*[72] is a good consolidated list which has the virtue of being relatively up-to-date, while R. W. Ball's bibliography[73] covers the more restricted field of the earlier stone age.

Retrospectively, the bibliographies of A. J. H. Goodwin,[74] although now out-of-date, remain definitive and useful for the earlier years. The bibliographies given in J. Desmond Clark's *Prehistory of Southern Africa*[75] and in R. J. Mason's *Prehistory of the Transvaal*[76] are two key sources which should not be overlooked.

---

71 Council for Old World Archaeology. Cowa Surveys and Bibliographies: South Africa, Area 13, No. IV, 1969; compiled by H. J. Deacon. Cambridge, Massachusetts, The Council, 1969.

72 HOLM, S. E. *Bibliography of South African Pre- and Proto-Historic Archaeology*. Pretoria. Van Schaik, 1966. (National Council for Social Research. Publication No. 16).

73 BALL, R. W. *The Earlier Stone Age in Southern Africa*: a Bibliography. Cape Town, University, School of Librarianship, 1964.

74 GOODWIN, A. J. H. *The Loom of Prehistory: a Commentary and a Select Bibliography of the Prehistory of Southern Africa*. Cape Town, South African Archaeological Society, 1946.

75 CLARK, J. D. *The Prehistory of Southern Africa*. Harmondsworth, Penguin Books, 1959.

76 MASON, R. J. *Prehistory of the Transvaal*. Johannesburg, Witwatersrand University Press, 1962.

572 ANTHROPOLOGY

One of the best basic bibliographies in this area is I. Schapera's *Select Bibliography of South African Native Life and Problems*[77] which is a critically annotated bibliography of books, periodicals, articles and government reports, and covers such topics as law, economics, education, religion, health and social services in so far as these relate to the Non-White peoples of the country. The important section on modern status and conditions has been supplemented by three bibliographies published by the University of Cape Town.[78] The basic work and the supplements have been reprinted in one volume by Kraus Periodicals Inc., New York.

A number of bibliographies dealing with specific aspects and specific races have also been published [79]

580 BOTANY

South Africa's rich floral heritage has received considerable attention bibliographically at various times, the most recent notable occasion being the Golden Jubilee of the National Botanic Gardens in 1963. At this time, the South African

---

77   SCHAPERA, I. *Select Bibliography of South African Native Life and Problems.* London, Oxford University Press, 1941.

78   1st Supplement (1939-1949) by M. A. HOLDEN and A. J. JACOBY, published 1950; 2nd Supplement (1950-1958) by J. BACK, and R. GIFFEN, published 1960; 3rd Supplement by C. SOLOMON (1958-1963), published 1964.

79   For example : ELLIS, B. L. *Religion among the Bantu in South Africa: Works Published after 1956.* Johannesburg, University of the Witwatersrand, Department of Bibliography, Librarianship and Typography, 1968;
DE JAGER, E. J. *A Select Bibliography of the Anthropology of the Cape Nguni Tribes.* Johannesburg, Public Library, 1966.

Library issued a bibliography[80] of some 244 books and 31 periodicals, principally of historically significant material. In this connection mention should be made of the bibliography[81] published by the Cape Town City Libraries for the same occasion. The early period is well covered by the 1882 Catalogue[82] of P. Macowan and H. Bolus.

590 ZOOLOGY

Most zoological monographs published in South Africa are well equipped with extensive bibliographies, but a good many bibliographies on specific subjects have been published separately, for example: M. G. Hughes on snakes,[83] H. J. Zwarenstein and others on Xenopus Laevis,[84] J. V. McIntosh on Mosquitoes of the genus Aedes,[85] and D. Sprenger on

---

80   South African Library, Cape Town. *Flora Africana: South African Botanical Books, 1600-1963: a Selective Bibliography*: compiled by W. TYRRELL-GLYNN with the Assistance of M. R. LEVYNS. Cape Town, The Library, 1963. (Grey Bibliographies, No. 8.)

81   Cape Town, City Libraries. 1963: *South Africa's Floral Year: a list of books . . .* compiled by J. GRIEVE. Cape Town, The Library, 1963.

82   MACOWAN, P. and BOLUS, H. 'Catalogue of Printed Books and Papers relating to South Africa . . . Botany.' In: *South African Philosophical Society. Transactions.* v.2, No. 3, 1882, p. 111-187.

83   HUGHES, M. G. The Snakes of Southern Africa: a Bibliography. Cape Town, University, School of Librarianship, 1952. Unpublished.

84   ZWARENSTEIN, H. J. AND OTHERS. *Xenopus Laevis: a Bibliography*. Cape Town, African Bookman, 1946. Supplement 1955 published by Medical Library, University of Cape Town.

85   MCINTOSH, J. V. *Mosquitoes of the Genus Aedes occurring in Southern Africa: a Bibliography*. Johannesburg, University of the Witwatersrand, Department of Bibliography, Librarianship and Typography, 1968.

animal distribution in Southern Africa.[86]

A good example of a bibliography published regularly by a scientific society is the *Limnological Bibliography for Africa South of the Sahara* which has appeared in each issue of the *Newsletter of the Limnological Society of Southern Africa* since No. 3 (August 1964).

610   MEDICINE

Burrows' *History of Medicine in South Africa*[87] has a comprehensive bibliography. J. Beckerling has covered a specific medico-historical topic with her bibliography[88] on the medical history of the Anglo-Boer War. Mention should also be made of the fifty year bibliography[89] covering the publications of the South African Institute for Medical Research, Johannesburg, 1913-1964.

Numerous bibliographies on specific topics also exist. Among the subjects covered are: Bilharzia[90] by E. Schoeman

---

86   SPRENGER, D. *Animal Distribution in Southern Africa.* Johannesburg, University of the Witwatersrand, Department of Bibliography, Librarianship and Typography, 1968.

87   BURROWS, E. H. *A History of Medicine in South Africa up to the end of the 19th Century.* Cape Town, Balkema, 1958. p. 370-377.

88   BECKERLING, J. L. *Medical History of the Anglo-Boer War: a Bibliography.* Cape Town, University, School of Librarianship, 1967.

89   South African Institute for Medical Research. *Publications, 1913-1964.* Johannesburg, The Institute, 1966.

90   SCHOEMAN, E. Bilharzia South of the Sahara, 1940-Sept. 1958: a Bibliography. Cape Town, University, School of Librarianship, 1959; Unpublished Zimerman, Z. *Bilharzia in Africa South of the Sahara, 1958-1966: a Bibliography.* Johannesburg, University of the Witwatersrand, 1967.

and Z. Zimerman; Cancer[91] by M. de Leeuw and S. N. Hebert; Poliomyelitis[92] by J. B. A. Janisch; Tuberculosis[93] by Z. D. Vickerstaff and P. Vidal; Virus and Rickettsial diseases[94] by M. Mersky and Medical Research on the Bantu, 1920-1957[95] by E. S. Ginsberg, M. Schwartz and S. Katcher.

630 AGRICULTURE

As agriculture plays an important part in the South African economy, agricultural topics have often received the

---

91 Bibliography on Cancer in Africa. Supplement to *South African Cancer Bulletin*. Main Bibliography (by M. de Leeuw) in v.7, *No. 4*, Oct./Dec. 1963;
    1st Supplement (by M. de Leeuw) in v.9, *No. 1*, Jan./Mar. 1965;
    2nd Supplement (by S. N. Hebert) in v.11, *No. 1*, Jan./Mar. 1967;
    3rd Supplement (by S. N. Hebert) in v.12, *No. 4*, Oct./ Dec. 1968.

92 JANISCH, J. B. A. A Bibliography of Poliomyelitis in Southern Africa, 1940-1958. Cape Town, University, School of Librarianship, 1958. Unpublished.

93 VICKERSTAFF, Z. D. *Tuberculosis in South Africa, 1940-1952: Bibliography*. Cape Town, University, School of Librarianship, 1952; VIDAL, P. Tuberculosis in South Africa, 1953-1959: a Bibliography. Cape Town, University, School of Librarianship, 1959. Not published.

94 MERSKY, M. Publications on Human Virus and Rickettsial Diseases from the Union of South Africa, 1947-1957: a Bibliography. Cape Town, University, School of Librarianship, 1960. Unpublished.

95 GINSBERG, E. S. and SCHWARTZ, M. *Medical Research on the Bantu in South Africa, 1920-Sept. 1952: a Bibliography*. Cape Town, University, School of Librarianship, 1954;
    KATCHER, S. *Medical Research on the Bantu in South Africa, Oct. 1952-Sept. 1957: a Bibliography*. Cape Town, University, School of Librarianship, 1958.

attention of bibliographers. Examples are: Cereals[96] by R. Flinn; Citrus fruit industry[97] by F. A. Stoy and R. G. Webb; Deciduous fruit[98] by M. G. Smith; Forestry[99] by J. Hubbard; Karakul sheep[100] by E. R. Kahn; Merino wool[101] by A. W. Rabe; Ostriches[102] by E. K. Mitchell; Sheep farming[103] by S. J. McDonald; Soil[104] by M. Luscombe; Sugar[105] by M. W. Rowley and Tobacco farming[106] by A. K. Krohn.

700 ART

R. F. Kennedy's five-volume *Catalogue of Pictures in the*

96   FLINN, R. *Cereals in South Africa: a Select Bibliography*. Cape Town, University, School of Librarianship, 1949.

97   STOY, F. A. *The Citrus Fruit Industry in South Africa: a Bibliography*. Cape Town, University, School of Librarianship, 1964; WEBB, R. G. *The Citrus Fruit Industry in South Africa: a Bibliography*. Cape Town, University, School of Librarianship, 1952.

98   SMITH, M. G. *Deciduous Fruit: a Bibliography*. Cape Town, University, School of Librarianship, 1950.

99   HUBBARD, J. *South African Forestry since 1913: a Bibliography*. Cape Town, University, School of Librarianship, 1950.

100 KAHN, E. R. *Karakul Sheep in South West Africa and South Africa: a Bibliography*. Cape Town, University, School of Librarianship, 1960.

101 RABE, A. W. *Merino Wool Production and Wool Research: a Bibliography*. Cape Town, University, School of Librarianship, 1952.

102 MITCHELL, E. K. *The Ostrich and Ostrich Farming: a Bibliography*. Cape Town, University, School of Librarianship, 1960.

103 MCDONALD, S. J. *Sheep Farming in South Africa since 1955*. Cape Town, University, School of Librarianship, 1968.

104 LUSCOMBE, M. *Soil: a Bibliography*. Cape Town, University, School of Librarianship, 1949.

105 ROWLEY, M. W. *Sugar: a Select Bibliography*. Cape Town, University, School of Librarianship, 1949.

106 KROHN, A. K. *Tobacco Farming in South Africa*. Cape Town, University, School of Librarianship, 1964.

Africana Museum, Johannesburg,[107] is a landmark in the
South African art history field, reproducing as it does each
of the six thousand pictures in the Africana Museum, and
giving bibliographical sources wherever possible. This work
is a mine of bio-bibliographical art information, as is also
A. Gordon-Brown's *Pictorial Art in South Africa*[108] which
covers the period to 1900. Mr. Kennedy's brief critical
review[109] of important South African art books which
formed part of an address he gave to the 1966 Conference
of the South African Library Association, should not be
overlooked. The bibliography[110] by D. M. Mirvish is an
attempt to cover twentieth century South African artists.
The Johannesburg Public Library maintains a card file of
exhibition and other references relating to South African
artists. A few important South African artists such as
Pierneef[111] and Bowler[112] have received bibliographical
attention in their own right.

South African sculpture has been the subject of two bibliographies by J. Bouman[113] and H. A. Louw.[114] E. Green has
treated the subject of African tribal sculpture[115] in a more

107 KENNEDY, R. F. *Catalogue of Pictures in the Africana Museum,*
     Johannesburg. The Museum, 1966-68. 5v.

108 GORDON-BROWN, A. *Pictorial Art in South Africa during Three
     Centuries to 1873.* London, Sawyer, 1952.

109 KENNEDY, R. F. 'Books; or, A Librarian in Retirement.' In:
     South African Libraries. v.34, No. 3, Jan. 1967, p. 111-119.

110 MIRVISH, D. B. *South African Artists, 1900-1958: a Biblio-
     graphy.* Cape Town, University, School of Librarianship,
     1960.

111 SMIT, S. J. H. Pierneef; the South African Artist: a Biblio-
     graphy. Cape Town, University, School of Librarianship,
     1957. Unpublished.

112 BRADLOW, F. R. *Thomas Bowler: His Life and Work.* Cape
     Town, Balkema, 1967.

recent bibliography. L. J. P. Gaskin's bibliography[115a] covers
a wider field.

720 ARCHITECTURE

The early period is well covered by R. Lewcock in his standard work[116] on early nineteenth century South African
architecture. Later South African architecture remains only
diffusely covered by a few bibliographies. E. O. Hewitt and
J. M. Rawson have compiled bibliographies[117] for the period
to 1952, while J. Nel and H. Wolff have covered the period
1950 to 1963 in more recent bibliographies.[118]

---

113   BOUMAN, J. Painting and Sculpture in South Africa: a Bibliography. Cape Town, University, School of Librarianship,
1945. Unpublished.

114   LOUW, H. A. South African Sculpture, 1910-1959: a Bibliography. Cape Town, University, School of Librarianship,
1959. Unpublished.

115   GREEN, E. *African Tribal Sculpture: a Bibliography.* Cape
Town, University, School of Librarianship, 1967.

115a GASKIN, L. J. P. *Bibliography of African Art.* London, International Affairs Institute, 1965.

116   LEWCOCK, R. *Early Nineteenth Century Architecture in South
Africa: a Study of the Interaction of Two Cultures, 1795-
1837.* Cape Town, Balkema, 1963. p. 437-442.

117   HEWITT, E. O. *A Bibliography of Architecture in South Africa
[to] 1945.* Cape Town, University, School of Librarianship,
1950;
RAWSON, J. M. *A Bibliography of Architecture in South Africa
from 1945.* Cape Town, University, School of Librarianship,
1952.

118   NEL, J. *Architecture in Africa South of the Sahara, 1952-1962.*
Johannesburg, University of the Witwatersrand, Department
of Bibliography, Librarianship and Typography. Unpublished;
WOLFF, H., *Architecture South of the Sahara: a List of References.* Johannesburg, University of the Witwatersrand.
Department of Bibliography, Librarianship and Typography,
1967.

737 NUMISMATICS

F. V. Noble's bibliography[119] covers the period from earliest times to 1965.

780 MUSIC

F. Z. van der Merwe's bibliography[120] is basic for white South African composers, while D. H. Varley's bibliography[121] and a later compilation[121a] by L. J. P. Gaskin cover African native music over a wider area.

792/9 THEATRE AND SPORT

F. C. L. Bosman's stage and drama bibliography[122] is basic for the earlier period, 1652-1855, while the bibliographies[123] by M. C. Veldsman and G. Emmerson cover the later period.

South Africa being a sport-loving country, bibliographies have covered most of the major sports. Examples are: W.

---

119 NOBLE, F. V. *South African Numismatics, 1652-1965: a Bibliography.* Cape Town, University, School of Librarianship, 1967.

120 VAN DER MERWE, F. Z. *Suid-Afrikaanse Musiekbibliografie, 1787-1952.* Pretoria, van Schaik, 1958. Supplemented in: *Africana Notes and News.* v.14, No. 7, Sep. 1961, p. 278-281; v.16, No. 6, June 1965, p. 238-274; v.17, No. 7, Sep. 1967, p. 328-336.

121 VARLEY, D. H. *African Native Music: an Annotated Bibliography.* London, Royal Empire Society, 1936. Reprinted London, Dawson, 1970.

121a GASKIN, L. J. P. *Select Bibliography of Music in Africa.* London, International African Institute, 1965.

122 BOSMAN, F. C. L. *Drama en Toneel in Suid-Afrika.* Deel 1, 1652-1855. Amsterdam, de Bussy, 1928.

123 VELDSMAN, M. C. Theatre in South Africa: a Bibliography. Cape Town, University, School of Librarianship, 1956. Unpublished; EMMERSON, G. Theatre in South Africa, 1956-1963: a Bibliography. Cape Town, University, School of Librarianship, 1964. Unpublished.

D

A. Malherbe on hockey,[124] M. A. M. Hart on cricket,[125] D. L. Rance on rugby football,[126] J. I. Campbell and M. P. Richards on mountaineering[127] and F. G. H. Whiteley on riding.[128]

820   SOUTH AFRICAN ENGLISH LITERATURE

E. Seary's *Biographical and Bibliographical Record of South African Literature in English*[129] although published as long ago as 1938 remains useful for the brief bibliographies given for each author. M. Nathan's bibliographical essay[130] is even older but remains useful in the absence of other suitable works. The South African P. E. N. Club published three year books and a fifty-year survey[131] which are useful

---

124   MALHERBE, W. A. *Chronological Bibliography of Hockey*. Johannesburg. Public Library, 1965.

125   HART, M. A. M. Bibliography on South African Cricket, 1810-1953. Cape Town, University, School of Librarianship, 1954. Unpublished.

126   RANCE, D. L. Bibliography on the History of South African Rugby, 1862-1955. Cape Town, University, School of Librarianship, 1956. Unpublished.

127   CAMPBELL, J. I. *A Bibliography of Mountains and Mountaineering in Africa*. Cape Town, University of Librarianship, 1950; RICHARDS, M. P. *Mountaineering in Southern Africa: a Bibliography*. Johannesburg, University of the Witwatersrand, 1966.

128   WHITELEY, F. G. H. *Riding Horse Types in South Africa, 1940-1960: a Bibliography*. Cape Town, University, School of Librarianship, 1962.

129   SEARY, E. R. *A Biographical and Bibliographical Record of South African Literature in English*. Grahamstown, The Author, 1938.

130   NATHAN, M. *South African Literature: a General Survey*. Cape Town, Juta, 1925.

131   South African P.E.N. Year Book, 1954-1957, 1960. Johannesburg, South African Centre of the International P.E.N. Club. 1960 entitled: P.E.N. 1960 includes a fifty year survey of South African English Literature.

bibliographically and the *Cambridge Bibliography of English Literature*[132] is another source which should not be overlooked for the early period to 1914 by virtue of its South African content. Mendelssohn's *South African Bibliography*, which has been mentioned previously is strong in literature in its classified section.

Current bibliographical coverage for South African English is given annually in *English Studies in Africa*.[133]

Prominent South African authors who have been made the subject of full-length bibliographies include Roy Campbell,[134] Nadine Gordimer,[135] Dan Jacobson,[136] Uys Krige,[137] Doris Lessing,[138] Sarah Gertrude Millin[139] and Olive Schreiner.[140]

---

132   *Cambridge Bibliography of English Literature*; ed. by F. W. BATESON. Cambridge, University Press, 1940. v.3, p. 1088-1093. v.5: Supplement, 1957, p. 707-708.

133   English Studies in Africa. Johannesburg, Witwatersrand University Press, 1958-.

134   DAVIS, V. *Bibliography of the Works of Ignatius Roy Dunnachie Campbell*. Cape Town, University, School of Librarianship, 1954.

135   NELL, R. J. *Nadine Gordimer: Novelist and Short Story Writer: a Bibliography*. Johannesburg, University of the Witwatersrand, Department of Bibliography, Librarianship and Typography, 1964.

136   YUDELMAN, M. *Dan Jacobson*. Johannesburg, University of the Witwatersrand, Department of Bibliography, Librarianship and Typography, 1967.

137   PLAISTOWE, Z. M. *Uys Krige: a Bibliography*. Cape Town, University, School of Librarianship, 1958.

138   IPP, C. *Doris Lessing: a Bibliography*. Johannesburg, University of the Witwatersrand, Department of Bibliography, Librarianship and Typography, 1967.

139   WHYTE, M. *Bibliography of the Works of Sarah Gertrude Millin*. Cape Town, University, School of Librarianship, 1953. New bibliography by F. LEVY in preparation at University of Witwatersrand.

140   VERSTER, E. Olive Emilie Albertina Schreiner: a Biblio-

Although no all-embracing consolidated and up-to-date bibliography exists for South African English, just as no handbook exists for South African English usage, bibliographies for various literary forms have been compiled from time to time:

Fiction: Among the earliest and best known bibliography in this field is J. P. L. Snyman's *Bibliography of South African Novels in English, 1880-1930*,[141] which formed the concluding part of the author's D. Litt. thesis at the Potchefstroom University and entitled *The Achievement of the South African Novel in English: a critical study.* This bibliography has been supplemented by A. Astrinsky's *Bibliography of South African English Novels, 1930-1960.*[142] The historical novel in South Africa has been treated bibliographically by S. Kiersen[143] and that of the Anglo-Boer War (1899-1902) by D. J. Weinstock.[144] The latter includes all known translations and a checklist of Dutch and Afrikaans novels as well. M. B. Hobson's Bibliography[145] covers eighty years of the

graphy. Cape Town, University of Cape Town, School of Librarianship, 1949.

141   SNYMAN, J. P. L. *A Bibliography of South African Novels in English Published from 1880-1930.* Potchefstroom, University, 1951.

142   ASTRINSKY, A. *A Bibliography of South African English Novels, 1930-1960.* Cape Town, University, School of Librarianship, 1965.

143   KIERSEN, S. *English and Afrikaans Novels on South African History: a Bibliography.* Cape Town, University, School of Librarianship, 1958.

144   WEINSTOCK, D. J. *Boer War in the Novel in English, 1884-1966: a Descriptive and Critical Bibliography.* Los Angeles, University of California, 1968. Published by University Microfilms in Xerox. Order No. 68-16954.

145   HOBSON, M. B. A Select Bibliography of South African Short Stories in English, 1870-1950. Cape Town, University, School of Librarianship, 1952. Unpublished.

South African short story. Each issue of the Index to *South African Periodicals* includes a list of short stories published in periodicals.

Drama: R. Silbert's *Southern African Drama in English*[146] has filled a considerable gap in this field. The Catalogue of the National Drama Library, Bloemfontein,[147] does include South African plays as well as overseas material.

Poetry: K. Wolpert is compiling a bibliography of South African English Poetry, 1937-1967.[148] G. Muller's *Bibliography of Poetical Works of Guy Butler, Anthony Delius and Roy Macnab*,[149] deals with three leading poets and is one of the few bibliographical sources in this special field. The *Index to South African Periodicals* includes a list of poems published in South African periodicals.

An up-to-date and detailed review of the whole field of South African English literature is given in R. Musiker's paper: 'South African English Literature: Bibliographical and Biographical Resources and Problems', which appeared in *English Studies in Africa*, v.13, No. 1, Mar. 1970, p. 265-73.

839.4 AFRIKAANS LITERATURE

Mention has already been made of the great contribution to

---

146 SILBERT, R. *Southern African Drama in English: an Annotated Bibliography*. Johannesburg, University of the Witwatersrand, 1965.

147 National Drama Library. Basic Catalogue. Bloemfontein, The Library, 1966.

148 WOLPERT, K. *South African English Poetry, 1937-1967: a Bibliography*. In Preparation at University of Witwatersrand, Department of Bibliography, Librarianship and Typography.

149 MULLER, G. A Bibliography of the Poetical Works of Guy Butler, Anthony Delius and Roy Macnab, as Published in Anthologies and South African Periodicals. Johannesberg, University of the Witwatersrand, 1962.

Afrikaans bibliography by Professor P. J. Nienaber through
his bibliography of Afrikaans books for the period from
1861 to the present time. Since 1947 the same author has
published a bibliography of periodical articles on Afrikaans
language and literature arranged by subjects.[150] A bibliography of Afrikaans short stories[151] was published in 1960,
and the Johannesburg Public Library compiled an index to
Afrikaans poetry[152] which was published in 1951. A supplement to this index is in preparation. As is the case with
South African English literature, a number of Afrikaans
authors have formed the subject of bibliographies. They
include: J. F. E. Celliers,[153] I. D. du Plessis,[154] C. J. Langenhoven,[155] C. L. Leipoldt,[156] W. E. G. Louw,[157] D. F. Malherbe,[158] E. N. Marais,[159] Mikro (C. H. Kuhn),[160] D. J.

150   NIENABER, P. J. *Bronnegids by die Studie van die Afrikaanse
      Taal en Letterkunde.* Johannesburg, The Author, 1947-.

151   MORRIS, G. R. *Kortverhaalregister: 'n Repertorium van Afri-
      kaanse Kortverhale, Novelles, Sketse en Vertellings.* Pretoria,
      Transvaal Provincial Library, 1960.

152   Johannesburg Public Library, *Register van Afrikaanse Poësie.*
      Pretoria, Van Schaik, 1957. Supplement in preparation.

153   GRIESSEL, M. *Bibliografie van Jan F. E. Celliers.* Cape Town,
      University, School of Librarianship, 1953.

154   VAN ZYL, S. M. *Izak David du Plessis: a Bibliography.* Cape
      Town, University, School of Librarianship, 1963.

155   MALAN, E. M. *Cornelis Jacob Langenhoven: Bibliografie.* Cape
      Town, University, School of Librarianship, 1953.

156   DU TOIT, S. W. R. *Christiaan Frederick Louis Leipoldt: Biblio-
      grafie.* Cape Town, University, School of Librarianship, 1949.

157   JOOSTE, M. C. Bibliografie oor W. E. G. Louw. Stellenbosch,
      University, Department of Librarianship, 1967. Unpublished.

158   ROUX, E. C. D. F. Malherbe: Bibliografie. Cape Town, Univer-
      sity, School of Librarianship, 1953. Unpublished.

159   ROSSOUW, F. *Eugène Nielsen Marais: Bibliografie.* Cape Town,
      University, School of Librarianship, 1958.

160   FERREIRA, P. T. *Mikro (Christoffel Hermanus Kuhn).* Cape
      Town, University, School of Librarianship, 1964.

Opperman,[161] M. E. Rothmann,[162] Totius (J. D du Toit),[163] C. M. van den Heever,[164] E. van Heerden[165] and N. P. van Wyk Louw.[166]

Other literary groups

J. A. Poliva's monograph[167] is a major bibliographical source for South African Jewish literature while J. Beinash has provided a bibliographical record of South African Jewish writers, 1940-1962,[168] and A. Wilkov has covered English writings by Non-Europeans (i.e. Non-White peoples) in South Africa, 1944-1960,[169] supplementing an earlier compilation[170] by N. M. Greshoff.

910 GEOGRAPHY AND TRAVEL

The most comprehensive bibliography of South African

---

161 MEISENHOLL, E. *Diederik Johannes Opperman: 'n Bibliografie.* Cape Town, University, School of Librarianship, 1964.

162 SMART, G. B. *Bibliografie van die Werke van M. E. R. (M. E. Rothmann).* Cape Town, University, School of Librarianship, 1960. Unpublished.

163 DU TOIT, A. S. *Bibliografie van Totius (Prof. Dr. J. D. du Toit).* Cape Town, University, School of Librarianship, 1950.

164 KAMP, Y. *Christiaan Mauritz van den Heever: Bibliografie.* Cape Town, University, School of Librarianship, 1953.

165 GOOSEN, P. *Ernst van Heerden.* Johannesburg, University of the Witwatersrand, 1963.

166 BARRATT, C. *N. P. van Wyk Louw: Bibliografie.* Cape Town, University, School of Librarianship, 1960.

167 POLIVA, J. A. *A Short History of the Jewish Press and Literature of South Africa.* Vereeniging, The Author, 1961.

168 BEINASH, J. *Books and Pamphlets by South African Jewish Writers, 1940-1962: a Bibliography.* Johannesburg, University of the Witwatersrand, 1965.

169 WILKOV, A. *Some English Writings by Non-Europeans in South Africa, 1944-1960: a Bibliography.* Johannesburg, University of the Witwatersrand, 1962.

170 GRESHOFF, N. M. *Some English Writings by South African Bantu.* Cape Town, University, School of Librarianship, 1949.

geography was compiled by H. C. Schunke-Hollway[171] and covers the period 1503 to 1888. P. Paulitschke's bibliography[172] covering the years 1500 to 1750, published in Vienna, is also basic.

N. H. MacKenzie's study[173] of South African travel literature in the seventeenth century has a fine bibliography on the subject, while R. G. Stephen has covered[174] eighteenth century travellers. Two bibliographies of personal accounts of early travellers by L. J. Engels[175] and K. L. M. Schmidt[176] cover the period 1652-1715 and 1715-1850 respectively. Although published abroad, a work basic to this section is E. G. Cox's *Reference Guide to the Literature of Travel*,[177] of which the first volume includes a lengthy section on

---

171   SCHUNKE-HOLLWAY, H. C. 'Bibliography of Books, Pamphlets, Maps, Magazine Articles, etc. relating to South Africa, with Special Reference to Geography from 1503 to 1888.' In: *South African Philosophical Society. Transactions.* v.10, No. 2, 1898, p. 131-294.

172   PAULITSCHKE, P. *Die Afrika-Literatur . . . 1500 bis 1750.* Vienna, Brockhausen, 1882. Reprinted: New York, Kraus, 1962.

173   MACKENZIE, N. H. 'South African Travel Literature in the 17th Century.' In: *Archives Yearbook for South African History,* 1955, Part 2, p. 1-112.

174   STEPHEN, R. G. Travellers in South Africa in the 18th Century. Cape Town, University, School of Librarianship, 1947. Unpublished.

175   ENGELS, L. J. 'Personal Accounts of the Cape of Good Hope Written between 1652 and 1715.' In: *Africana Notes and News.* v.8, No. 3, June 1951, p. 71-100.

176   SCHMIDT, K. L. M. *A Bibliography of Personal Accounts of the Cape of Good Hope in Printed Books, 1715-1850.* Cape Town, University, School of Librarianship, 1956.

177   COX, E. G. *A Reference Guide to the Literature of Travel.* Seattle, University of Washington, 1935-38. v.1: The Old World. p. 354-401: Africa.

Africa. Two other overseas publications which appear annually include a brief section of South African material in each issue. They are the *Bibliographie Cartographique Internationale*[178] and the *Bibliographie Géographique Internationale*.[179] The specific topic of Shipwrecks off the South African Coast has been well covered by R. F. Kennedy.[180] A supplement by D. H. Selesnik is in preparation at the University of the Witwatersrand Department of Bibliography, Librarianship and Typography.

912 MAPS

V. S. Forbes has done sterling pioneer work in this field. In a major contribution on the early period he has provided an excellent bibliographical essay[181] on South African maps between 1595 and 1795. The section on maps in S. Mendelssohn's *South African Bibliography*[182] remains a most useful tool in this field. The Johannesburg Public Library's *Descriptive Catalogue of Decorative Maps of Africa up to 1800*[183]

---

178 *Bibliographie Cartographique Internationale*. Paris, Armand Colin, 1946-.

179 *Bibliographie Géographique Internationale*. Paris, Centre National de la Recherche Scientifique, 1891-.

180 KENNEDY, R. F. *Shipwrecks on and off the coasts of Southern Africa: a Catalogue and Index*. Johannesburg, Public Library, 1955. Supplement by D. H. Selesnik in preparation at University of the Witwatersrand, Department of Bibliography, Librarianship and Typography.

181 FORBES, V. S. 'Some Early Maps of South Africa, 1595-1795.' In: *Journal for Geography* (Stellenbosch), v.2, No. 6, Apr. 1965, p. 9-20.

182 MENDELSSOHN, S. *South African Bibliography*. London, Kegan Paul, 1910. v.2, p. 1095-1113.

183 Johannesburg Public Library. *Exhibition of Decorative Maps of Africa Up to 1800, 4-16 August 1952: Descriptive Catalogue*. Johannesburg, The Library, 1952.

also remains an excellent source of bibliographical information on this subject as is also the map section in the 1952 Van Riebeeck Anniversary publication South Africa in Print.[184]

Two bibliographies of maps of Southern Africa in printed books compiled by J. F. and M. F. Cartwright[185] between them covered the period 1500-1856. The two bibliographical studies of R. V. Tooley[186] and D. Schrire[187] on early maps of the Cape of Good Hope were published abroad but they are two of the few to have ventured bibliographically into the South African map scene. Denis Godfrey has provided a brief informal background to the field in his book *The Enchanted Door*.[188]

In so far as present-day maps are concerned, the Scientific Council for Africa has published two bibliographical handbooks[189] dealing with topographical and subject maps respectively.

---

184   Van Riebeeck Festival, 1952: *South Africa in Print*. Cape Town, Book Exhibition Committee, 1952.

185   CARTWRIGHT, J. F. A Bibliography of Maps of Southern Africa in Printed Books, 1750-1856; Cartwright, M. F. A Bibliography of Maps of Africa and Southern Africa in Printed Books, 1500-1750. Cape Town, University, School of Librarianship, 1955. Both unpublished.

186   TOOLEY, R. V. *Early Maps and Views of the Cape of Good Hope: an illustrated Commentary*. London, Map Collectors' Circle, 1963. (Map Collectors' Series, No. 6.)

187   SCHRIRE, D. *The Cape of Good Hope, 1782-1842, from De La Rochette to Arrowsmith; being some Notes on the Development of the Early Mapping of European Occupied South Africa by English Cartographers*. London, Map Collectors' Circle, 1965. (Map Collectors' Series, No 17.)

188   GODFREY, D. *The Enchanted Door: a Discourse on Africana Book-Collecting*. Cape Town, Timmins, 1963. p. 220-236.

189   Scientific Council for Africa South of the Sahara. *Topographical Maps of Africa South of the Sahara, Part 1; Maps of*

Current lists[190] of South African maps are published biennially by the Government's Advisory Survey Council.

920 BIOGRAPHY

A bibliography of collective South African biography[191] has been compiled by Le Roux Olivier. R. Ushpol has compiled a bibliography of South African autobiographies,[192] while M. J. Stern has covered South African Jewish Biography.[193] A number of bibliographies of famous South African personalities, chiefly statesmen, also exist. Examples include: Louis Botha,[194] J. B. M. Hertzog,[195] L. S. Jameson,[196] D. F. Malan,[197] C. J. Rhodes,[198] C. J.

Africa South of the Sahara. Part 2: Special Subject Maps. London, Commission for Technical Co-operation in Africa South of the Sahara, 1955.

190 South Africa (Republic). National Advisory Survey Council. *Catalogue of Maps Published in the Republic of South Africa.* Pretoria, Government Printer.

191 OLIVIER, LE ROUX. *Versamelde Suid-Afrikaanse Biografieë: n Bibliografie.* Cape Town, University, School of Librarianship, 1963.

192 USHPOL, R. *A Select Bibliography of South African Autobiographies.* Cape Town, University, School of Librarianship, 1959.

193 STERN, M. J. *South African Jewish Biography.* Cape Town, University, School of Librarianship, 1967.

194 CLARK, E. M. M. *Louis Botha: a Bibliography.* Cape Town, University, School of Librarianship, 1959.

195 BURGER, M. J. *Generaal J. B. M. Hertzog: 'n Bibliografie.* Cape Town, University, School of Librarianship, 1953.

196 COOPER, P. J. Dr. Jameson: a Bibliography. Cape Town, University, School of Librarianship, 1951. Unpublished.

197 WILLIAMS, L. E. *Dr. Daniel Francois Malan, 1874-1959: a Bibliography.* Pretoria, University of South Africa, Department of Bibliography and Library Science, 1967.

198 BURKE, E. E. *A Bibliography of Cecil John Rhodes, 1853-1902.* Salisbury, Central African Archives, 1953; THOMSON, D. W.

Smuts[199] and Margaret Ballinger.[200]

968 HISTORY

Three professors of history have jointly compiled a select bibliography of South African history.[201] This is a checklist of 2521 items, unfortunately not annotated.

G. W. Eybers' *Select Constitutional Documents Illustrating South African History*[202] is a key source book for the period 1795 to 1910. The standard histories of South Africa have fairly comprehensive bibliographies. Examples are: *Cambridge History of the British Empire*, volume eight,[203] C. F. Muller's *Five Hundred Years*,[204] A. J. H. Van der Walt's *Geskiedenis van Suid-Afrika*[205] and E. A. Walker's *History of Southern Africa.*[206] F. A. van Jaarsveld's writing[207] is also

Cecil John Rhodes: a Bibliography. Cape Town, University, School of Librarianship, 1949.

199   GREENWALD, D. J. Jan Christiaan Smuts: Bibliography. Cape Town, University, School of Librarianship, 1951. Unpublished.

200   UDEMAN, E. *The Published Works of Mrs. Margaret Livingstone Ballinger: a Bibliography*. Johannesburg, University of the Witwatersrand, 1968.

201   MULLER, C. F. J. AND OTHERS. *A Select Bibliography of South African History*. Pretoria, University of South Africa, 1966. (Communications of the University of South Africa, D3).

202   EYBERS, G. W. *Select Constitutional Documents illustrating South African History, 1795-1910.* London, Routledge, 1918.

203   *Cambridge History of the British Empire.* Cambridge, University Press, v.8, 2nd ed. 1963. p. 917-1017.

204   MULLER, C. F. J. ed. *Five Hundred Years: a History of South Africa.* Pretoria, Academica, 1969.

205   VAN DER WALT, A. J. H. AND OTHERS, eds. *Geskiedenis van Suid-Afrika;* 2de uitgawe. Kaapstad, Nasou, 1965. p. 593-607.

206   WALKER, E. A. *A History of Southern Africa.* 3rd ed. London, Longmans, 1957. p. 925-945.

207   VAN JAARSVELD, F. A. *The Afrikaner's Interpretation of South African History,* Cape Town, Simondium, 1964.

well equipped bibliographically. Specific periods in South
African history have also been covered bibliographically. A
few examples are: J. G. Kesting on the Anglo-Boer War,[208]
I. Grivainis on the Great Trek,[209] and B. A. Verner on the
Huguenots.[210]
The Constitutional development of South Africa has been
dealt with bibliographically in two compilations by J.
Hutton[211] and A. Towert.[212]

REGIONAL BIBLIOGRAPHIES

South Africa: Examples of regions and towns covered bibliographically are: Durban[213] by B. M. Bee; East London[214] by
D. E. Gray; Grahamstown[215] by J. Fisher and M. Hartzen-

---

208 KESTING, J. G. *The Anglo-Boer War, 1899-1902 . . . a Bibliography.* Cape Town, University, School of Librarianship,
1956.

209 GRIVAINIS, I. *Material Published after 1925 on the Great Trek
until 1854.* Cape Town, University, School of Librarianship,
1967.

210 VERNER, B. A. *Huguenots in South Africa.* Cape Town, University, School of Librarianship, 1967.

211 HUTTON, J. *The Constitution of the Union of South Africa: a
Bibliography.* Cape Town, University, School of Librarianship, 1950.

212 TOWERT, A. M. F. *Constitutional Development in South
Africa, 1946-1959: a Bibliography.* Cape Town, University,
School of Librarianship, 1960; reprinted 1963.

213 BEE, B. M. *Historical Bibliography of the City of Durban or
Port Natal to 1939.* Cape Town, University, School of Librarianship, 1949.

214 GRAY, D. E. A Select Bibliography on East London. Cape
Town, University, School of Librarianship, 1954. Unpublished.

215 FISHER, J. E. Grahamstown, 1812-1910: a Bibliography. Cape
Town, University, School of Librarianship, 1954. HARTZEN-
BERG, M. Grahamstown: a Bibliography. Grahamstown,
Rhodes University Library, 1968. Both unpublished.

berg; Kimberley[216] by D. Robins; Orange Free State[217] by
M. C. E. van Schoor and S. I. Malan; Orange Free State Gold-
fields[218] by D. M. Sinclair; Orange River[219] by D. J. Muller;
Pietermaritzburg[220] by M. Vowles; Pietersburg[221] by E.
Davidson; Port Elizabeth[222] by G. N. Price; Pretoria[223] by
K. E. Cross; Stellenbosch[224] by H. I. Rudd and Zululand by
M. H. Galloway[225] and J. F. Duggan.[226]

South West Africa: The most comprehensive and up-to-date
bibliography on South West Africa is T. de Jager's compila-

216   ROBINS, D. E. Kimberley: a Bibliography. Grahamstown,
      Rhodes University library, 1968. Unpublished.
217   VAN SCHOOR, M. C. E. and MALAN, S. I. *'n Bibliografie van
      Werke oor die Oranje-Vrystaat van af die vroegste tye tot
      1910.* Bloemfontein, The Compilers, 1954.
218   SINCLAIR, D. M. *The Orange Free State Goldfields: a Biblio-
      graphy.* Cape Town, University, School of Librarianship,
      1967.
219   MULLER, D. J. *The Orange River: a Bibliography.* Cape Town,
      University, School of Librarianship, 1953.
220   VOWLES, M. *The City of Pietermaritzburg: a Bibliography.*
      Cape Town, University, School of Librarianship, 1949.
221   DAVIDSON, E. *Pietersburg Magisterial District.* Johannesburg,
      University of the Witwatersrand, Department of Biblio-
      graphy, Librarianship and Typography, 1968.
222   PRICE, G. N. *A Bibliography of Port Elizabeth.* Cape Town,
      University, School of Librarianship, 1950.
223   CROSS, K. E. *Bibliography of Pretoria.* Cape Town, University,
      School of Librarianship, 1950.
224   RUDD, H. I. Bibliography of Stellenbosch, 1679-1850. Cape
      Town, University, School of Librarianship, 1954. Unpub-
      lished.
225   GALLOWAY, M. H. *Zululand and the Zulus: a Bibliography.*
      Cape Town, University, School of Librarianship, 1944. Re-
      printed 1963.
226   DUGGAN, J. F. Zululand and the Zulus: a Bibliography. Cape
      Town, University, School of Librarianship, 1964. Unpub-
      lished.

tion[227] for the State Library. This was published in 1964 and had some 2000 references to books and pamphlets on all aspects of South West Africa. The work is arranged alphabetically by author and complemented by a detailed subject index. This bibliography represents a consolidation of all the entries in earlier bibliographies, but the following two compilations, which between them cover the period 1919-1960, remain useful by virtue of their subject arrangement: F. J. Welch, *South West Africa, 1919-1946*[228] and E. J. Roukens de Lange, *South West Africa, 1946-1960.*[229] A good many references to South West Africa are also recorded in O. H. Spohr's bibliography on German Africana described in Chapter One. A bibliography[230] by L. I. Botha on the Namib Desert has recently been completed.

Botswana, Lesotho and Swaziland: The three former High Commission Territories are well-covered bibliographically. *Botswana (formerly Bechuanaland):* Two bibliographies by P. E. Stevens[231] and C. Middleton[232] (1965) between them cover this territory in 305 and 155 entries respectively.

227 DE JAGER, T. *comp. South West Africa.* Pretoria, State Library, 1964. (State Library. Bibliographies, No. 7.)

228 WELCH, F. J. *South West Africa 1919-1946: a Bibliography.* Cape Town, University, School of Librarianship, 1949; reprinted 1967.

229 ROUKENS DE LANGE, E. J. *South West Africa, 1946-1960: a Selective Bibliography.* Cape Town, University, School of Librarianship, 1962.

230 BOTHA, L. I. *The Namib Desert: a Bibliography.* Cape Town, University, School of Librarianship, 1967.

231 STEVENS, P. E. *Bibliography of Bechuanaland.* Cape Town, University, School of Librarianship, 1949; reprinted 1964.

232 MIDDLETON, C. *Bechuanaland: a Bibliography.* Cape Town, University, School of Librarianship, 1965.

Another bibliography[233] on this territory has been compiled by P. Mohome and J. B. Webster at Syracuse University, New York.

Lesotho (formerly Basutoland): J. te Groen's bibliography[234] was published in 1946. M. E. Roth is compiling a bibliography[235] on the territory which provides up-to-date coverage. A bibliography on this territory, compiled at Syracuse University, New York, was published in 1968.[236]

Swaziland: J. Arnheim's bibliography (150 entries)[237] compiled in 1950 has recently been superseded by a more recent compilation[238] by C. S. Wallace consisting of 1191 entries. This is twice as extensive as the Bibliography[239] recently published at Syracuse University.

233   MOHOME, P. and WEBSTER, J. B. *A Bibliography on Bechuanaland.* Syracuse, N.Y. Syracuse University. Maxwell Graduate School of Citizenship and Public Affairs Program of East African Studies, 1966. Supplement 1968.

234   TE GROEN, J. C. *Bibliography of Basutoland.* Cape Town, University, School of Librarianship, 1949; reprinted 1964.

235   ROTH, M. E. *Bibliography of Lesotho.* In Preparation at University of the Witwatersrand, Johannesburg.

236   WEBSTER, J. B. and MOHOME, P. *A Bibliography on Lesotho.* Syracuse, N.Y. Syracuse University, Maxwell Graduate School of Citizenship and Public Affairs, Program of Eastern African Studies, 1968.

237   ARNHEIM, J. *Swaziland: a Bibliography.* Cape Town, University, School of Librarianship, 1950; reprinted 1963.

238   WALLACE, C. S. *Swaziland: a Bibliography.* Johannesburg, University of the Witwatersrand, Department of Bibliography, Librarianship and Typography, 1967.

239   WEBSTER, J. B. and MOHOME, P. *A Bibliography on Swaziland.* Syracuse, N.Y., Syracuse University, Maxwell School of Citizenship and Public Affairs, Program of Eastern African Studies, 1968.

Transkei: The bibliography[240] given in *South Africa's Transkei* by G. M. Carter *and others* is the most comprehensive on this territory.

Angola: M. J. Greenwood's bibliography[241] on this neighbouring African territory, also much in the news, has the virtue of being up-to-date and covers numerous aspects, including economics, geography, ethnology, history, missions, politics and social conditions.

Great emphasis has been laid in this Chapter on South African imprints, but the role of important sources originating from countries outside South Africa should not be overlooked.

In his book on *Australian Bibliography,*[242] D. H. Borchardt singles out the *Subject Catalogue of the Royal Empire Society* (four volumes, 1930-37) as being a valuable source in these terms:

'No student of Australia can get far without being thoroughly familiar with this bibliographical catalogue of one of the best collections on the subject outside Australia.'

It is no exaggeration to say the same of that part of the first volume of the *Catalogue* which deals with South Africa, especially as bibliography in South Africa experienced a lean period between the two World Wars.

Likewise the research worker in Britain who wishes to have

---

240 CARTER, G. M. AND OTHERS. *South Africa's Transkei.* London, Heinemann, 1967. p. 189-200.

241 GREENWOOD, M. J. *Angola: a Bibliography.* Cape Town, University, School of Librarianship, 1967.

242 BORCHARDT, D. H. *Australian Bibliography;* 2nd ed. Melbourne, Cheshire, 1966. p. 4.

E

a bibliographical guide to material available in the United Kingdom on South Africa will find A. R. Hewitt's *Guide to Resources for Commonwealth Studies in London, Oxford and Cambridge*[243] a valuable contribution especially for history and social science, The subject catalogue of the Rhodes House Library, Oxford, will shortly be photographed and published.

In recent years the amount of bibliographical lists and guides appearing abroad have multiplied to such an extent that it is no longer possible to list them all in the present work. Attention to this matter, and to the most important overseas sources, has already been drawn[244] by A. R. Taylor in the U.S.A., and by R. Musiker in his paper *A World View of Africana* delivered at the first South African Conference of Bibliophiles in 1966 and since published in South Africa[245] and the United Kingdom.[246] The compilations of the Library of Congress, Washington, deserve special mention and have been listed[247] by J. W. Witherell.

---

243   HEWITT, A. R. *Guide to Resources for Commonwealth Studies in London, Oxford and Cambridge, with Bibliographical and other Information.* London, Athlone Press, 1957.

244   TAYLOR, A. R. 'Library and Archival Resources for African Studies: Present State and Future Needs.' Paper presented to 11th Annual Meeting of African Studies Association, Los Angeles, Oct. 16-19, 1968.

245   MUSIKER, R. A World View of Africana. In: *Bibliophilia Africana, 1966.* Cape Town, Friends of the South African Library, 1967, p. 19-24.

246   MUSIKER, R. 'A World View of Africana.' In: *Library Materials on Africa.* v.5, No. 2, Nov. 1967, p. 48-55.

247   WITHERELL, J. W. 'Bibliographical Programs on Africa in Washington, D.C., at the Library of Congress and the African Bibliographic Center.' Paper presented to the International Conference on African Bibliography, Nairobi, Dec. 1967.

4 | Periodicals and Newspapers: Indexes and Lists

INDEXES

The importance of a periodicals index in making a nation's writing fully accessible to research workers and librarians needs no restatement here. Periodicals without indexes are rendered virtually useless. Considerable attention has therefore been paid by the library profession in South Africa to the matter of an adequate index to periodicals.

The *Index to South African Periodicals*[1] which covers the period from 1940 to date is an example of a most successful enterprise in this field. The Johannesburg Public Library has been responsible for the work for all except the first two years of its existence and has done a remarkably fine job.

The *Index* covers 300 of the more important South African periodicals. Scholarly journals especially in science and technology are fully indexed and the more general and popular ones are selectively indexed. Certain literary reviews and original literary contributions are also included.

Annual volumes appear soon after the year has ended and these are cumulated decennially. Decennial volumes for 1940/1949 (4 volumes) and 1950/1959 (3 volumes) exist.

An examination of the *Index* reveals that it consists chiefly of articles of particular South African relevance, that is, articles dealing with local problems, conditions, events and personalities. It is, for example, an indispensable guide to information on the Non-White peoples of South Africa and the Native races of Africa in general. While it is true that the

---

1   *Index to South African Periodicals, 1940/49.* Johannesburg, Public Library.

scientific and technological articles in an index of this kind have a South African slant, there is also a wealth of material, the subject matter of which is not limited by any South African association. James Winter, who has written an excellent descriptive article[2] on the scope of the *Index*, stresses this point:

'A reference librarian makes a great mistake if he only consults the *Index* when dealing with inquiries which have a specifically South African slant. Only to consult the *Index to South African Periodicals* for items with a South African slant is to miss some of the fine research done locally especially in fields where local research is strong, for example, the mining industry and agriculture.'

The fact that the *Index* is only published once a year is a disadvantage in tracing the most recent material, although the compilers of the *Index* willingly answer written enquiries about recent material, as yet unpublished.

South African librarians and many abroad as well have rejoiced in the news that the Johannesburg Public Library has launched a project to index the periodical literature of South Africa for the years 1900-1939. A start was made early in 1966, and great progress has been made since then.

LISTS
In 1965 the State Library published a classified list of some 1200 current South African periodicals,[3] and this has been supplemented annually. This directory supersedes a directory of similar scope published by the South African Library as

---

2   WINTER, J. S. 'The Index to South African Periodicals.' In: *South African Libraries.* v.34, No. 3, Jan. 1967, p. 85-89.

3   State Library, Pretoria. *Current South African Periodicals: a classified List, July 1965.* Pretoria, The Library, 1966. (State Library. Bibliographies. No. 8.) Annual Supplements.

Grey Bibliography No. 5[4] in 1951, and to some extent also Grey Bibliography No. 4[5] which dealt with annuals. A directory of South African periodicals in scientific and technical fields has been published by the Council for Scientific and Industrial Research.[6]

The importance of a union list of all serials (not only those published in South Africa) held in South African libraries is as vital for inter-library loan activities as for the research worker.

A. C. G. Lloyd's *Catalogue* published in 1912 (see p. 85) was the first venture in this field in South Africa and since then the union list of serials has had a curious history. In 1943 P. Freer started a *Catalogue of Union Periodicals*,[7] adopting an unusual catchword arrangement which resulted in a very cumbersome tool. This work was eventually published in two volumes covering Science/Technology and Humanities respectively. Two Supplements to the Science Volume were issued in 1949 and 1953. By 1961 the Council for Scientific and Industrial Research and the National Council for Social Research had launched a new venture entitled *Periodicals in South African Libraries*,[8] which D. H. Varley has

---

4 South African Library, Cape Town. *Handlist of South African Periodicals . . . Current in December 1951*. Cape Town, The Library, 1951.

5 South African Library, Cape Town. *Classified List of South African Annual Publications as at March 31st 1961*. Cape Town, The Library, 1951.

6 South African Council for Scientific and Industrial Research. *Directory of Scientific and Technical Periodicals Published in South Africa*. Pretoria, The Council, 1967-.

7 FREER, P. *ed. Catalogue of Union Periodicals*. Pretoria, Council for Scientific and Industrial Research and National Council for Social Research, 1943-52. 2v. Supplements 1-2 to Vol. 1.

8 Periodicals in South African Libraries: a Revised Edition of the Catalogue of Union Periodicals. Pretoria, South African Council for Scientific and Industrial Research and National Council for Social Research, 1961-.

called the greatest co-operative achievement in South African library history. The aim of this work like Freer's earlier *Catalogue of Union Periodicals* (or *C.U.P.* as it is commonly known) is to list holdings and locations of all serials found in South African libraries. Unlike Freer's work, *Periodicals in South African Libraries* (or *P.I.S.A.L.* as it is generally abbreviated) appears in loose-leaf form, is arranged alphabetically by the title of the periodical and subject to continuous revision. The work had reached the letter P at July 1969. Plans have been announced to expedite the completion of the project i.e. letters Q to Z, and to implement a speedy continuous revision service by means of computerized methods.

The aim, scope and method of compilation of *P.I.S.A.L.* has been described by one of the compilers.[9]

Pending the completion of the basic volume of *P.I.S.A.L.*, other smaller union lists in selected subject areas remain useful, and will undoubtedly continue to be useful even after *P.I.S.A.L.* is complete because the subject approach of these smaller lists are in fact complementary to the alphabetically arranged *P.I.S.A.L.* The State Library has published union lists covering library science,[10] anthropology and archaeology,[11] sociology[12] and classical antiquity.[13] There are also separate union lists

 9   DE GRAAF, A. M. 'Periodicals in South African Libraries (P.I.S.A.L.)' In: *South African Libraries.* v.31, No. 1, Jul. 1963, p. 13-16.
10   ASCHENBORN, H. J. comp. *Library Journals in South African Libraries.* Pretoria, State Library, 1960. (Bibliographies, No. 1.)
11   ASCHENBORN, H. J. comp. *Anthropological Journals in South African Libraries.* Pretoria, State Library, 1961. (Bibliographies, No. 2.)
12   ASCHENBORN, H. J. comp. *Sociological Journals in South African Libraries.* Pretoria, State Library, 1961. (Bibliographies, No. 3.)
13   SCHOEMAN, E. comp. *Periodicals on Classical Antiquity and Related Subjects.* Pretoria, State Library, 1963. (Bibliographies, No. 5.)

available for medicine[14] and mathematics.[15] The Johannesburg Public Library's list of *African Serial Publications Currently Received*[16] is of special value because the pan-African serial holdings of this major South African library are among the best on the African Continent.

The State Library is at present preparing a list of ceased South African periodicals.

NEWSPAPER INDEXES AND LISTS

It is indeed regrettable that there is at present no retrospective or current index to South African newspapers. While the Newspaper Press Union decided in October 1967 not to give financial support to a retrospective index of any South African newspapers, against the recommendations of the library profession in South Africa, efforts are still being made to launch at least a current index to a South African newspaper. Language problems in a bilingual country and the high cost of maintaining such an index have been two of the factors which impeded progress in this venture.

The State Library is preparing a list of current South African newspapers. One of the few important lists in this field is the South African Library's *Union List of South African Newspapers*,[17] published in 1950 as Grey Bibliography No. 3. Entries

---

14 ROBINOW, B. H. *comp. Union List of Periodicals in Medical Libraries in South Africa*. Durban, University of Natal, 1963.

15 South African Council for Scientific and Industrial Research. National Research Institute for Mathematical Sciences. *Periodicals with Mathematical Content in South African Libraries*. Pretoria, The Institute, 1969.

16 Johannesburg Public Library. *African Serial Publications Currently Received, as at March 1967*; compiled by A. CLIFTON. Johannesburg, The Library, 1967.

17 South African Public Library, Cape Town. *Union List of South African Newspapers, November 1949*. Cape Town, The Library, 1950. (Grey Bibliographies, No. 3.)

in this list are arranged alphabetically by place of publication complemented by an index of newspaper titles. Information given includes date of first issue, date ceased, changes of title and locations with holdings. Although now out-of-date it remains a useful list. T. Cutten's *History of the Press in South Africa*[18] provides a useful bibliographical background.

The State Library is also preparing directories of current and ceased South African newspapers. In so far as current newspapers are concerned, the *Advertising and Press Annual of Africa*[19] continues to provide reasonably good coverage. Most of the overseas publications, which list South African newspapers, for example, *Willing's Press Guide* and *Writers' and Artists' Year Book*, cover only a small proportion of the newspapers published in South Africa.

One of the most formidable Government Commission Reports issued in recent times was that of the Press Commission under the chairmanship of Dr. J. W. van Zyl in ten volumes.[20] From the bibliographer's point of view, Appendix Eight is of greatest interest because of the list of South African newspapers published therein. Some of the other volumes have a critical analysis of the newspapers themselves.

A list of South African newspapers and periodicals available on microfilm has been published in an overseas publication.[21]

---

18 CUTTEN, T. E. G. *History of the Press in South Africa*. Cape Town, National Union of South African Students, 1935.

19 Advertising and Press Annual of Africa. Cape Town, National Publishing Co., 1949-.

20 South Africa (Union). Commission of Inquiry into the Press. Condensed Report. Pretoria, Government Printer, 1961.

21 State Library, Pretoria. 'South African Newspapers and Periodicals Available on Microfilm, September 1963. In: *Africana Newsletter* (Hoover Institution, Stanford, California) v.2, No. 2, 1964, p. 48-51.

The Johannesburg Public Library has published a union list of non-South African newspapers held in South African Libraries.[22]

---

22 Johannesburg Public Library. *Union List of Non-South African Newspapers in South African Libraries;* edited by M. Galgut. Johannesburg, The Library, 1965.

5 | Theses and Research

The documentation of work done as theses and dissertations in South Africa presents a favourable picture. Not only do several consolidated bibliographies exist, but the work is kept current.

Two bibliographies cover the period 1918-1958. A. M. Lewin Robinson's *Catalogue of Theses and Dissertations . . . 1918-1941*[1] lists some 1757 titles. S. I. Malan's *Union Catalogue of Theses and Dissertations*[2] covers the years 1942-1958. Both works have the virtue of serving as a union list and give location of copies.

The primary arrangement in both works is by subjects, but whereas Robinson's bibliography is sub-arranged by author, Malan's work is sub-arranged by university and then only by author. Both bibliographies have full author indexes, but only Robinson gives a specific subject index. The absence of such an index in Malan's work makes its use awkward from the point of view of the reader approaching by subject.

Potchefstroom University, which published Malan's Catalogue, has published annual supplements[3] since 1959, but these appear some time after the end of the year, and the absence of a cumulation after ten years is a further drawback to the efficient use of this tool.

---

1 ROBINSON, A. M. LEWIN. *Catalogue of Theses and Dissertations Accepted for Degrees by the South African Universities, 1918-1941*. Cape Town, The Author, 1943.

2 MALAN, S. I. *Union Catalogue of Theses and Dissertations of the South African Universities, 1942-1958*. Potchefstroom, Potchefstroom University for C.H.E., 1959.

3 Potchefstroom University for C.H.E. *Ferdinand Postma Library. Union Catalogue of Theses and Dissertations of the South African Universities, 1959-*. Potchefstroom, The Library. Annual.

The consolidated list of theses of the University of South Africa[4] deserves to be mentioned because there are entries in this work which have been omitted from the lists compiled by Robinson and Malan. The reason for this situation is that the University of South Africa for many years had a number of constituent university colleges under its control and the theses produced at these colleges, which later became fully-fledged universities, have been listed more comprehensively in this bibliography than in those by Robinson and Malan. The Universities of Potchefstroom, Pretoria, and Orange Free State publish annual lists of theses accepted for degrees, while others publish such lists less frequently. In addition, many South African university calendars also have lists of theses.

Two major sources cover current research at South African universities. The humanities are covered by the *Register of Current Research in the Human Sciences*[5] published annually since 1949 by the National Council for Social Research,* but this tool affords only partial coverage of humanities and social science research. The scientific equivalent of this work is however more comprehensive. This is the *Register of Current Scientific Research at South African Universities*,[6] which has been compiled and published annually by the Council for

---

4 University of South Africa. *List of Dissertations and Theses Accepted by the University of South Africa, 1919-1958.* Pretoria, The University, 1958. Supplemented by Summaries of Theses Accepted . . . 1959-.

5 South Africa (Republic). National Council for Social Research. *Register of Current Research in the Human Sciences at the Universities.* Pretoria, The Council, 1949-.

6 South African Council for Scientific and Industrial Research. *Register of Current Scientific Research at South African Universities.* Pretoria, The Council, 1951-.

*Now the Human Sciences Research Council.

Scientific and Industrial Research since 1951. Entries in both registers are arranged by subject disciplines and sub-arranged by universities. Both works give the title and brief description of the project, the names of investigators and the probable duration of research.

6 | Official Publications

D. H. Borchardt defines[1] Official Publications as documents
emanating from government agencies and relating to adminis-
trative activities of such agencies in relation to the national
scene. Political, social and economic history are reflected in a
government's documentation. Furthermore, as I. Isaacson has
pointed out,[2] there is often a wealth of valuable and interesting information hidden between the dull covers of an official
publication, and if official documents have never become best-
sellers in this country, lack of publicity may be partly to
blame.

As in the case of Australia, British administration of South
Africa in earlier times resulted in a wealth of British reports
on affairs in South Africa, which have often been called
Imperial Blue Books. A number of bibliographies, search lists
and guides to the materials of South African interest in the
Public Records Office now exist. Some of these lists have
recently been published in micro-form.[3] Further checklists
of relevant files and 'Blue Books' are given in the Cambridge

1   BORCHARDT, D. H. *Australian Bibliography: a Guide to Printed
    Sources of Information.* 2nd ed. Melbourne, Cheshire, 1966. p.
    53.

2   ISAACSON, I. 'The Official Publications of the Union of South
    Africa.' In: *South African Libraries.* v.7, No. 4. Apr. 1940, p.
    162.

3   Great Britain. Public Records Office. (1) List of Colonial Office
    Records as at January 1962. London, H.M.S.O., 1964. (2) Cata-
    logue of Microfilm. 1967.

4   *Cambridge History of the British Empire;* 2nd ed. Cambridge
    University Press, 1963. v.8, p. 928-959.

History of the British Empire,[4] volume eight; in E. A. Walker's *History of Southern Africa*[5] and in Giuseppi's *Guide*.[6]

In addition to Colonial Office publications it should be remembered that British Parliamentary Papers also included South African material. P. and G. Ford have edited several select lists and breviates of these Parliamentary Papers for the years 1833-1899 for the Irish Universities Press, as well as Hansard's *Catalogue and Breviate of Parliamentary Papers, 1696-1834*.[7] British Reports of Debates in the House of Commons, and the Papers and Journals of the House of Commons also have numerous South African associations and source material for historical research.

A well-known source which remains useful is M. I. Adam's *Guide to the Principal Parliamentary Papers Relating to the Dominions, 1812-1911*,[8] long out of print. South Africa is included in this work.

The bibliographical situation regarding official publications in South Africa has never been very satisfactory. Although the South African Library Association has expressed dissatisfaction at various times, it has not succeeded in solving the problem entirely. On the other hand, if one can judge by the example set in other countries, then the fault lies with the Government Printer who, in South Africa, has never issued a comprehensive catalogue of publications.*

---

5   WALKER, E. A. *A History of Southern Africa*; 3rd ed. London, Longmans, 1957.

6   GIUSEPPI, M. S. *Guide to the Contents of the Public Records Office*. London, H.M.S.O., 1963. 2 v.

7   Full details of these reprints are given in the Catalogue of the Irish Universities Press.

8   ADAM, M. I. AND OTHERS. *Guide to the Principal Parliamentary Publications Relating to the Dominions, 1812-1911*. Edinburgh, Oliver & Boyd, 1913, p. 89-146.

*   The first volume of a *Bibliography of South African Government Publications* covering Statistics, 1910-1968, was published by the Government Printer, Pretoria in February 1970.

In so far as retrospective bibliography is concerned, one major tool[9] exists for the period 1910 to 1961. This is the only guide of its kind to government publications, but it has so many omissions and a questionable *ad-hoc* arrangement by subject catchwords, that its use is very limited. The compilers in the House of Assembly responsible for the work deny that the work was ever intended for an audience wider than Parliamentary personnel. Nevertheless, in the absence of any other tool for the period it remains useful. D. L. Ehlers has contributed a paper[10] on its use.

The period since 1961 has been well covered in the two national bibliographies (*Africana Nova* and the *South African National Bibliography*), but the Government Printer himself issues no more than a monthly mimeographed *List of Official Publications*, which is also reprinted in the *Government Gazette*, usually weekly. This list is never cumulated and the advantage of having a consolidated annual list, following the practice in the U.S.A. and the United Kingdom, is lost.

Government Commissions of Inquiry have a high recall value by the names of their Chairmen, yet this important finding device has been overlooked in all the official publication indexes from 1854 to 1961. It has in fact been left to an individual, I. Isaacson, to take it upon himself to compile two lists[11] of Government Commissions arranged by the names of

---

9 South Africa (Republic). House of Assembly. *Index to the Manuscript Annexures and Printed Papers of the House of Assembly including Select Committee Reports and Bills, and also to Principal Motions and Resolutions and Commission Reports, 1910-1961.* Cape Town, Government Printer, 1963.

10 EHLERS, D. L. 'A Method of Information Retrieval from South African Government Publications.' In: *South African Libraries.* v.31, No. 2, Oct. 1963, p. 66-68.

11 ISAACSON, I. 'A Finding List of South African Commissions and Committees of Enquiry under Names of Chairmen.' Part 1 in *South African Libraries.* v.20, No. 2, Oct. 1952, p. 42-48; Part 2 in *South African Libraries.* v.20, No. 3, Jan. 1953, p. 84-86.

Chairmen, but the years since 1952 remain uncovered in this respect, except for the contributions of the national bibliographies (since 1959).

Official publications are by their nature complex items to handle and difficult to use. I. Isaacson contributed two useful articles on Central[12] and Provincial[13] Government Publications respectively which remain useful and informative. This should be prescribed reading for any person faced with the prospect of working with South African official publications.

C. de B. Webb has compiled a comprehensive guide[14] to the official records of Natal, which is indispensable source material for this province, while P. J. Schutte has compiled a bibliography[15] of Transvaal official publications before Union i.e. 1881-1900.

The years prior to 1910 are covered in the Cape by two bibliographies. The Clerk of the Cape House of Assembly issued an *Index*[16] for the years 1854 to 1910 in three volumes, which are arranged even more unconventionally than the 1910/1961 Index already mentioned. R. and N. Musiker have compiled a chronological/numerical and subject index to Cape

---

12   ISAACSON, I. 'Official Publications in the Union of South Africa (excluding Provincial Administrations)' In: *South African Libraries.* v.7, No. 4, Apr. 1940, p. 155-162.

13   ISAACSON, I. 'Official Publications of the Provinces of the Union of South Africa, with a Bibliography.' In: *South African Libraries.* v.11, No. 2, Oct. 1943, p. 31-36.

14   WEBB, C. DE B. *A Guide to the Official Records of the Colony of Natal.* Pietermaritzburg, University of Natal Press, 1965.

15   SCHUTTE, P. J. 'n Beredeneerde Gesamentlike Katalogus van Groenboeke van die Zuid-Afrikaansche Republiek. Pretoria, State Library, 1966. (State Library. Bibliographies, No. 9.)

16   Cape of Good Hope. House of Assembly. Index to the Annexures and Printed Papers . . . 1854-1897; 1898-1903; 1904-1910. Cape Town, Cape Times, printers, 1899-1910. 3 v.

17   MUSIKER, R. and MUSIKER, N. *Cape Official Publications 1854-1910.* Pretoria, State Library. In the Press.

Official Publications, 1854/1910,[17] which is being published by
the State Library. In addition, S. Mendelssohn's *South African
Bibliography*[18] has an appendix listing official publications
(chiefly Imperial 'Blue Books'), and should not be overlooked
in any search for early items.

The bibliographies of official publications given in the
Official Year Book of the Union of South Africa from 1910-
1960 are important. These lists were not always repeated in
successive volumes. Consequently some of the Year Books have
more comprehensive bibliographies than others. The Bibliography given in the *Year Books* No. 1-12 for 1910-1929/30 are
especially noteworthy as they contained a consolidated bibliography for the years since Union (1910).

Besides the question of bibliography at Central and Provincial Government level, there is also the local and municipal
authority level to consider. In this respect, South Africa is for-
tunate in having a major public library, which for many years
has had a departmental library specialising in this field, viz.
the Municipal Reference Library of the Johannesburg Public
Library. This Library is particularly strong in South African
municipal publications and has published a useful bibliography[19] of South African municipal books and periodicals
received by the Library. Earlier bibliographies by L. P. Green,[20]
J. P. R. Maud[21] and A. B. Steele[22] remain useful.

---

18 MENDELSSOHN, S. *South African Bibliography*. London, Kegan
    Paul, 1910. v.2, p. 653-710.
19 Johannesburg. Public Library. *Southern African Municipal
    Publications: a List of Holdings in the Reference Libraries.*
    Johannesburg, The Library, 1965.
20 GREEN, L. P. *History of Local Government in South Africa.*
    Cape Town, Juta, 1957. p. 99-104.
21 MAUD, J. P. R. *City Government: the Johannesburg Experiment.*
    Oxford, Clarendon Press, 1938. Literature of Municipal Gov-
    ernment in South Africa, p. 386-397.
22 STEELE, A. B. Local Government in South Africa: a Biblio-
    graphy. Cape Town, University, School of Librarianship, 1947.
    Unpublished.

F

7 | Archives and Manuscripts

As is the case in most countries the Government Archives in South Africa fulfil a valuable role in historical research and house primary source material. Their primary function is the preservation of the official record of the Government and its departments, and the classification and organisation of this record for the use of the public.

A brief general account of the South African Archives was a regular feature of each edition of the *Official Year Book of the Union of South Africa*[1] until the descriptive part of this publication was discontinued in 1960. More recently, comprehensive accounts of archival activities are to be found in the *Annual Reports* of the Director of Archives. Articles on the history and development of archival agencies and work in South Africa have been published from time to time in the *South African Archives Journal*, the official organ of the South African Association of Archivists, since this journal first appeared in 1959. A good series of well-illustrated descriptive popular articles[2] about the Archives also exists.

Bibliographically, the Archives by their very nature present difficulties, in that very few countries can emulate the detailed search lists of the Public Records Office in Great Britain. Brief guides[3] do however exist for South Africa.

---

1   For example: The Public Archives of South Africa. In: *Official Year Book of the Union of South Africa*, No. 30, 1960, p. 286-290.

2   In: *Lantern*. v.7, Dec. 1957, p. 126-133 (Public Archives); v.7, Mar. 1958, p. 248-261 (Cape); v.8, Dec. 1958, p. 154-161 (Orange Free State); v.8, Mar. 1959, p. 268-279 (Natal); v.9, Dec. 1959, p. 142-153 (Transvaal) and v.9, Mar. 1960, p. 294-301 (Union Archives).

3   For example: BOTHA, C. G. *A Brief Guide to the Various*

In South Africa the Archives are decentralised and there are six depots, that is one for each Province, situated in Cape Town, Bloemfontein, Pietermaritzburg and Pretoria, a central depot in Pretoria and a depot for the territory of South West Africa in Windhoek. A consolidated list of finding aids to assist research workers is now available.[3a] This takes the form of a twenty-nine page list of the inventories, catalogues, indexes and registers housed in the archives depots. The material listed includes documents of government archives, magistrates' offices and local authorities, as well as private collections, maps, photographs and microfilms.

C. Graham Botha, one of the nation's best known former Chief Archivists has written copiously[4] on the Archives and some of his publications have taken the form of bibliographical guides to the Archives. T. W. Baxter has also done likewise[5] in a wider field covering Sub-Saharan Africa.

The Archives have issued a *List of Archives Publications published officially after 1925.*[6] This is a full list of Archives publications giving author, title and price, and including a full contents list of *Archives Year Book of South Africa* (from volume one, 1938 onwards) as well as a detailed list of *South African Archival Records* for each of the Provinces.

Classes of Documents in the Cape Archives for the Period 1652-1806. Cape Town, *Cape Times*, 1918.

3a South Africa (Republic) Archives. *List of Finding Aids in Archives Depots.* Pretoria, The Archives, 1969.

4 BOTHA, C. G. *Cape Archives and Records.* Cape Town, Struik, 1962.

5 BAXTER, T. W. *Archival Facilities in Sub-Saharan Africa.* London, Commission for Technical Co-operation in Africa South of the Sahara, 1959.

6 South Africa (Republic). Archives. *List of Archives Publications Published Officially after 1925.* Pretoria, The Archives, 1964.

F*

The South African Library, Cape Town, possesses the country's greatest single collection of manuscripts, a collection of unusually great variety. Many of these manuscripts have been edited and published at various times, principally in the *Quarterly Bulletin of the South African Library* and in the publications of the Van Riebeeck Society. A full bibliography of these manuscripts is still in the process of being compiled under the direction of W. Tyrrell-Glynn, the Deputy Librarian. He has in the meantime contributed a brief account[7] of the Library's diverse manuscript holdings to the volume published on the occasion of the national library's 150th anniversary. The same volume contains a complete list of the incunabula held by the Library: a collection unique in Southern Africa. There is however no union list of incunabula held in South Africa.

This Library has also since 1966 been engaged on the compilation of a national inventory of manuscript holdings, a task initiated at the request of the Bibliographical Committee of the South African Library Association. This project will include the collections in the care of cities, museums, churches and various other organisations, business firms and individuals. The material ranges in scope from family trees, diaries and war memoirs to letters and original drawings. All are invaluable in cultural, genealogical and historical research.

A major bibliographical source for manuscript material is Una Long's *Index to Authors of Unofficial, Privately owned Manuscripts relating to the History of South Africa, 1812-1920*,[8] which is a work mostly concerned with the English

---

7   TYRRELL-GLYNN, W. Die Handskrifte-Afdeling: Manuskrip materiaal van Suid-Afrikaanse Belang in die Biblioteek. In: The South African Library: its History, Collections and Librarians, 1818-1968; edited by C. Pama. Cape Town, Balkema, 1968. p. 85-97.
8   LONG, U. *An Index to Authors of Unofficial, Privately-Owned*

settlers of 1820 and their descendants.

Several important bibliographies of manuscript material have been published in recent years. Missionaries have always featured prominently in South African history, and P. Hinchliff has calendared[9] a considerable quantity of missionary correspondence in the Archives of the London Missionary Society, the United Society for the Propagation of the Gospel and the Methodist Missionary Society, for the years 1800-1850. In so far as particular denominations are concerned, a bibliography[10] of the manuscripts in the Methodist Archives, housed in the Cory Library for Historical Research, Rhodes University, Grahamstown, was published in 1968, while the University of the Witwatersrand had some years earlier produced a list[11] of the material in the Collection of the Church of the Province of South Africa housed in that Library.

The Universities in South Africa have taken great pride in cataloguing their manuscript collections. The University Libraries of Cape Town[12] and Witwatersrand[13] have both pub-

---

Manuscripts relating to the History of South Africa, 1812-1920, with Copies, Summaries and Extracts of Documents, Bibliographical Notes on the Authors, a Chronological Table and an Appendix of Documents originating outside South Africa. London, Lund Humphries, 1947.

9 HINCHLIFF, P. *Calendar of Cape Missionary Correspondence, 1800-1850.* Pretoria, National Council for Social Research, 1967. (Publication No. 27).

10 Rhodes University, Cory Library for Historical Research. *Methodist Archives Collection.* [Catalogue compiled by J. M. Berning]. Grahamstown, The Library, 1968.

11 Church of the Province of South Africa. Central Record Library. *Select Catalogue.* Johannesburg, The Library, 1960.

12 University of Cape Town Libraries. *Handlist of Manuscripts in the University of Cape Town Libraries, Part 1;* compiled by G. D. Quinn and O. H. Spohr. Cape Town, The Libraries, 1968. (Varia Series, No. 10).

13 University of the Witwatersrand. Library. *Guide to the*

lished bibliographies of their manuscript and archive collections recently, while the annual accession list of the Cory Library at Rhodes University has a section on manuscripts received in each issue. A list[14] of the extensive manuscript holdings of Rhodes House Library, Oxford, has also been published recently.

Archives and Papers held in the University Library. Johannesburg, The Library, 1967.

14   Rhodes House Library. *Manuscript Collections of Africana in Rhodes House Library, Oxford;* compiled by L. B. Frewer. Oxford, Bodleian Library, 1968.

8—Bibliography in South Africa

Although there are now well over three hundred public libraries and almost that number of special libraries in South Africa, relatively few engage in bibilographical work of the kind reflected in the contents of this book. It is of course true that nearly all libraries compile bibliographies in one form or another in the course of their day-to-day activities, but these compilations are generally of an order which cannot be considered as supplements to the nation's bibliographical equipment. It would hardly be fair to single out any libraries for special mention but perusal of the pages of this book reveals that a handful of libraries have taken the lead in producing bibliographical work of national importance.

ROLE OF INDIVIDUALS

The same is true of individual enterprise in South African bibliography. Bibliography in South Africa has forged ahead as much through the efforts of individual persons as through the work of institutions. South Africa has a great number of bibliophiles and collectors of Africana, but bibliographical contributions have to a large extent been the work of librarians with a special flair and enthusiasm for bibliography.

A few deserve special mention: A. C. G. Lloyd, Compiler of the first union list of periodicals[1] in South Africa, published in 1912; P. Freer, Editor of the *Catalogue of Union Periodicals*[2]

---

1   LLOYD, A. C. G. *Catalogue of Serial Publications Possessed by the Geological Commission of the Cape Colony, the Royal Observatory, South African Association for the Advancement of Science, South African Museum and South African Public Library.* Cape Town, South African Public Library, 1912.
2   FREER, P. *ed. Catalogue of Union Periodicals.* Pretoria, Council

and Author of *Bibliography and Modern Book Production;*[3]
R. F. Kennedy, Author of *Africana Repository*[4] and Compiler
of the *Catalogue of Pictures in the Africana Museum, Johan-
nesburg;*[5] Anna H. Smith who succeeded R. F. Kennedy as City
Librarian, Johannesburg and Director of the Africana Museum,
and who has maintained the same high standard of bibliographical work emanating from those two institutions; D. H.
Varley, founder of numerous South African bibliographical
ventures, Author of *Adventures in Africana*[6] and compiler of
Bibliographical Progress Reports, 1956-1961[7]; and A. M. Lewin
Robinson, author of *Systematic Bibliography,*[8] compiler of
Catalogue of Theses and Dissertations, 1918-1941[9] and editor
of *Bibliography of African Bibliographies,*[10] who succeeded

for Scientific and Industrial Research and National Council
for Social Research, 1943-1952.

3   FREER, P. *Bibliography and Modern Book Production: Notes
and Sources.* Johannesburg, Witwatersrand, University Press,
1954.

4   KENNEDY, R. F. *Africana Repository: Notes for a Series of Lec-
tures.* Johannesburg, Juta, 1965.

5   KENNEDY, R. F. *Catalogue of Pictures in the Africana Museum.*
Johannesburg, Africana Museum, 1966-1968. 5v.

6   VARLEY, D. H. *Adventures in Africana.* Cape Town, University,
1949.

7   VARLEY, D. H. 'Bibliographical Progress in Southern Africa.'
In: *South African Libraries.* 1956/58 In: v.26, No. 2, Oct.
1958, p. 55-60; 1958/59 In: v.27, No. 2, Oct. 1959, p. 58-64;
1959/60 In: v.28, No. 2, Oct. 1960, p. 49-55; 1960/61 In:
v.29, No. 2, Oct. 1961, p. 67-73, 78. (Title varies).

8   ROBINSON, A. M. LEWIN. *Systematic Bibliography.* London,
Bingley, 1966.

9   ROBINSON, A. M. LEWIN. *Catalogue of Theses and Dissertations
Accepted for Degrees by the South African Universities, 1918-
1941.* Cape Town, The Author, 1943.

10 South African Library, Cape Town. *Bibliography of African
Bibliographies,* 4th ed. Cape Town, The Library, 1961.

D. H. Varley as Chief Librarian of the South African Library; H. J. Aschenborn, Director of the State Library, under whose leadership the bibliographical work of this National Library has reached new heights in recent years; R. F. M. Immelman who has specialised in early Cape library history and bibliophiles; O. H. Spohr, prolific writer and bibliographer in the field of German Africana mentioned earlier in this book; S. I. Malan, Compiler of the *Union Catalogue of Theses and Dissertations 1942-1958;*[11] I. Isaacson, who contributed much to the documentation of official publications; G. R. Morris, compiler of a guide to Afrikaans subject literature[12] and compiler of the 1963 edition of *Reference Books for Public Library Use;*[13] and R. Musiker, whose *Guide to South African Reference Books*[14] is about to appear in a fifth edition, and who has tried to fill the 'reporting'[15] gap left by D. H. Varley.

The contributions of non-librarians have also been of great importance. For example, the contributions of W. H. Bleek, C. A. Fairbridge, G. McCall Theal and S. Mendelssohn to retrospective South African bibliography have already been mentioned in the present work. Professor P. J. Nienaber's bibliographies of Afrikaans language and literature described earlier remain unique, and the book-trade contributions of Nico S. Coetzee, compiler of the *South African Catalogue of Books,*

---

11 MALAN, S. I. *Union Catalogue of Theses and Dissertations of the South African Universities, 1942-1958.* Potchefstroom, University for C.H.E., 1959.

12 MORRIS, G. R. *Die Afrikaanse Vakliteratuur.* Pretoria, Transvaal Provincial Library, 1958.

13 MORRIS, G. R. *Reference Works for Public Library Use.* Pretoria, Transvaal Provincial Library, 1963.

14 MUSIKER, R. *Guide to South African Reference Books;* 4th ed. Cape Town, Balkema, 1965.

15 MUSIKER, R. 'Bibliographical Progress in South Africa, 1961/63-.' In: *South African Libraries.* See the end of this chapter for full details of this series of reports.

and of the publishing firm of C. Struik have also been mentioned.

Underlying the contributions of these individuals and institutions in South Africa has been the spirit of co-operation which exists at all levels. The two union lists of periodicals, the two union catalogues of theses and dissertations, and the Mendelssohn Revision Project are just a few examples of national tools which would have been impossible to realise without the co-operation of libraries throughout the country.

PRINCIPAL DEVELOPMENTS

Bibliographical work in South Africa received little attention from the pioneer library surveyors of the Carnegie Corporation in 1928 and the subsequent Interdepartmental Committee on the Libraries of the Union of South Africa in 1936.

It was not until 1943 that bibliographical activity took a great step forward at national level, for in this year the South African Library Association appointed a sub-committee to prepare a survey of existing bibliographical projects. This survey[16] was presented to the Association's 1943 Conference, and accepted as a basis for future bibliographical planning. Articles surveying the bibliographical scene were published by P. Freer[17] and H. Holdsworth[18] in 1945 and 1947 respectively.

In 1949 a bibliographical committee was appointed as a standing committee to serve as a national planning group, and reported annually thereafter on bibliographical progress. The material in the reports was later used by R. L. Collison in his

---

16　'Bibliographical Desiderata for South Africa: General Conspectus.' In: *South African Libraries.* v.11, No. 2, Oct. 1943, p. 39-40.
17　FREER, P. 'Bibliographical Work in South Africa.' In: *ASLIB 19th Conference Proceedings.* 1944, p. 44-48.
18　HOLDSWORTH, H. 'Bibliography in South Africa.' In: *Journal of Documentation.* v.3, Dec. 1947, p. 151-159. Supplemented in *Revue de Documentation.* v. 17, No. 6, Nov. 1950, p. 180.

publication *Bibliographical Services throughout the World*,[19] published by UNESCO.

At the Annual Conference of the South African Library Association held in Potchefstroom in 1959 an Action Committee was appointed to improve library co-operation, and the terms of reference of this Committee included a request for the planning of bibliographical services. D. H. Varley was subsequently appointed to survey the bibliographical scene and his report[20] was published in *Aspects of South African Libraries*. The South African Library Association used this report as a basis to formulate a number of recommendations.

These recommendations were presented at a National Conference of Library Authorities in Pretoria in November 1962, and the resolutions published in the form of a *Programme for Future Library Development in the Republic of South Africa.*[21]

The Conference recommended the establishment of a central body for bibliographic and information services to be known as the South African Bibliographical Bureau. The aims of the Bureau would be to plan, promote, co-ordinate and administer bibliographical services in South Africa, as well as to investigate, standardise and co-ordinate documentation and information services. A further goal would be to provide, promote, and administer research activities in these fields. Of the many sug-

---

19   COLLISON, R. L. *Bibliographical Services Throughout the World 1950-1959.* Paris, Unesco, 1961.

20   VARLEY, D. H. 'Report and Recommendations on Bibliographical Needs.' In: *Aspects of South African Libraries.* Potchefstroom, South African Library Association, 1962.

21   National Conference of Library Authorities, Pretoria, 1962. 'Programme for Future Library Development in the Republic of South Africa.' In: *South African Libraries.* v.30, No. 3, Jan. 1963, p. 81-117.

gestions made by the Conference, a few projects such as the compilation of an index to periodicals for the period prior to 1940 and a restrospective national bibliography for the period prior to 1959, have already been launched.

Implementation of other aspects of this Development Programme has been slow, chiefly because of the lack of financial support.

Although the Bureau envisaged by the 1962 Conference has still not been formed the South African Library Association has been very active in steering bibliographical activity, in launching new projects of national importance and in filling lacunae in the country's bibliographical apparatus. It was at the suggestion of this Committee that O. H. Spohr compiled a list[22] of existing known indexes to some seventy works of Africana which have had indexes compiled some time after original publication of the book. The Committee has met regularly and an annual report on its activities has been published in the Annual Report of the South African Library Association.

Mention has already been made of the importance of Africana in South African libraries with attendant implications for bibliography. It is beyond the scope of the present work to delve in depth into the ramifications of Africana, but it should be noted that several excellent works giving a background to Africana literature and bibliography already exist. R. F. Kennedy's *Africana Repository*[23] is one such work, while D. Godfrey has approached the subject from a journalist's point of view in two books, one of which deals with Africana book collecting[24] and the other[25] with Africana objects includes chapters on limited editions, recipe books, prints and art.

---

22   SPOHR, O. H. 'Recent Indexes to Africana Books.' In: *South African Libraries*. v.37, No. 1, Jul. 1969, p. 29-31.
23   KENNEDY, R. F. *Africana Repository*. Cape Town, Juta, 1965.

Two South African periodicals have been outstanding in their coverage of Africana topics. *Africana Notes and News*, published by the Africana Museum, Johannesburg, has appeared regularly since 1943 and the *Quarterly Bulletin of the South African Library* since 1946. Both periodicals have been indexed in the *Index to South African Periodicals*, and are themselves well equipped with cumulative indexes, which still further facilitate the use of these excellent tools as primary sources for bibliographical research in South Africa. An important event in Africana bibliography was the first South African Conference of Bibliophiles held in Cape Town in 1966. The Proceedings and Papers have been published.[26]

There have been a number of articles and papers in recent years which give bird's eye surveys of the bibliographical scene in South Africa. The most recent are R. Musiker's article[27] on Bibliography in the first volume of the *Standard Encyclopaedia of Southern Africa* and his paper:[28]

Bibliographical Achievement in South Africa presented at the International Conference on African Bibliography held in Nairobi in December 1967. This updates the same writer's

---

24 GODFREY, D. *The Enchanted Door: a Discourse on Africana Book-Collecting.* Cape Town, Timmins, 1963.

25 GODFREY, D. *Antiques and Bygones; Notes for South African Collectors.* Cape Town, Timmins, 1967.

26 Bibliophilia Africana, being the Proceedings of the First Conference of South African Bibliophiles held at the South African Library, Cape Town, Nov. 28-Dec. 1, 1966. Cape Town, Friends of the South African Library, 1967.

27 MUSIKER, R. Bibliography in South Africa. In: *Standard Encyclopaedia of Southern Africa.* Cape Town, Nasionale Pers. In the Press.

28 MUSIKER, R. 'Bibliographical Achievement in South Africa.' In: *The Bibliography of Africa;* edited by J. D. Pearson and Ruth Jones. London, F. Cass for International African Institute. In the Press.

survey[29] published four years earlier in 1963.

A first rate contribution[30] on the same theme, written by C. Reitz, a South African librarian now resident in Canada, was published in 1967. O. H. Spohr has written similiar papers[31] in German language periodicals from time to time.

Current bibliographical progress reports by R. Musiker appear in the *South African Library Association Newsletter* several times a year. More permanent reports,[32] usually biennial, also compiled by R. Musiker are published in *South African Libraries.*

29 MUSIKER, R. 'South African Bibliography: a Review.' In: *College and Research Libraries.* v.24, No. 6, Nov. 1963, p. 496-500.

30 REITZ, C. H. South African Bibliography. Illinois University, Graduate School of Library Science, 1967. (Occasional Papers, No. 90.)

31 For example: SPOHR, O. H. 'Wissenschaft in Afrika: süd Afrikanische Bibliographien der Afrikaforschung.' In: *Afrika Heute.* 15 Dec. 1963, p. 1-6; Entwicklung bibliographischer Arbeit in Südafrika Seit 1960. In: *Nachrichten für Dokumentation.* v. 19, No. 6, 1968, p. 251-254.

32 MUSIKER, R. 'Bibliographical Progress in South Africa.' Jul. 1961/Jun. 1963 In: *South African Libraries.* v.31, No. 2, Oct 1963, p. 49-58. Jul. 1963/Dec. 1964. In: *South African Libraries,* v33, No. 2, Oct. 1965, p. 55-64. Jan. 1965/Dec. 1966 In: *South African Libraries.* v.35, No. 2, Oct. 1967, p. 57-64. Jan. 1967/Dec. 1968 In: *South African Libraries.* v.37, No. 1, Oct. 1967, p. 57-64.
Jan. 1967/Dec. 1968 *In: South African Libraries.* v.37, No. 1, Jul. 1969, p. 13-19.

Index

Subjects are shown in capital letters.
Authors are indexed comprehensively; titles selectively.